From Darkness to Light

From Darkness to Light is translated from the French published by Éditions Olivétan as *Des ténèbres à la lumière*

In the same collection of translations:

The Silence of God during the Passion
Praying the Psalms
Spiritual Maladies
The Tenderness of God
Becoming a Disciple
Repentance—Good News!

From Darkness to Light

Daniel Bourguet

Foreword by Bob Ekblad

Translated from the French

CASCADE *Books* • Eugene, Oregon

FROM DARKNESS TO LIGHT

English translation Copyright © 2016 Wipf and Stock Publishers. All rights reserved. Except for brief quotations in critical publications or reviews, no part of this book may be reproduced in any manner without prior written permission from the publisher. Write: Permissions, Wipf and Stock Publishers, 199 W. 8th Ave., Suite 3, Eugene, OR 97401.

Translated from the original French edition.
Copyright © 2011 Éditions Olivétan, Lyon, France.

Cascade Books
An Imprint of Wipf and Stock Publishers
199 W. 8th Ave., Suite 3
Eugene, OR 97401

www.wipfandstock.com

PAPERBACK ISBN: 978-1-4982-8185-0
HARDCOVER ISBN: 978-1-4982-8187-4
EBOOK ISBN: 978-1-4982-8186-7

Cataloguing-in-Publication data:

Names: Bourguet, Daniel.

Title: Darkness to light / Daniel Bourguet.

Description: Eugene, OR: Cascade Books, 2016.

Identifiers: ISBN 978-1-4982-8185-0 (paperback) | ISBN 978-1-4982-8187-4 (hardcover) | ISBN 978-1-4982-8186-7 (ebook)

Subjects: LSCH: Jesus Christ—Crucifixion | Bible. Psalms, LXXXVIII—Criticism, interpretation, etc | Bible. Psalms—Devotional use | Jesus Christ—Resurrection | Hope—Religious aspects—Christianity | Mary Magdalene

Classification: BT453 B68 2016 (PRINT) | BT453 (EBOOK)

Manufactured in the U.S.A.   08/31/16

Contents

Translator's Note | vi
Foreword by Bob Ekblad | vii
Preface | xiii

1   Christ and the Thief (Luke 23:32–49) | 1
2   The Psalm of Descent into Hell (Psalm 88) | 43
3   Christ and Mary Magdalene (John 20:1–18) | 73

Translator's note

IN SOME INSTANCES THERE are idioms in French that are difficult to translate, but that has not generally been the case with this book. The author's original notes and references are all to French works or translations, and it has not always been possible to provide equivalent references in English. Further to the author's original notes some translator's notes have been added as footnotes, generally as glosses of the French, sometimes of a more explanatory nature; in every instance these notes have been checked with the author. Biblical passages are mostly the translator's version of the French since at times the point would be lost if this were not so; the author chooses freely among French translations.

Foreword

THE PUBLICATION OF DANIEL Bourguet's books in English is a valuable contribution to the literature of contemplative theology and spirituality that will nourish and inspire the faith of all who read them. Daniel Bourguet, a French Protestant pastor and theologian of the Huguenot tradition, lives as a monk in the mountainous Cévennes region in the South of France. There at his hermitage near Saint-Jean-du-Gard, Daniel maintains a daily rhythm of prayer, worship, Scripture reading, theological reflection, and spiritual accompaniment. All of his books flow out of a life steeped in love of God, Scripture, and the seekers who come to him for spiritual support.

I first met Daniel Bourguet in 1988 when my wife, Gracie, and I moved from rural Central America to study theology at the Institut Protestant de Théologie (IPT), where he taught Old Testament. The IPT is the Église protestante unie de France's[1] denominational graduate school in Montpellier, France.

Prior to our move to France while ministering among impoverished farmers in Honduras in the 1980s, we had come across the writings of Swiss theologian Wilhelm Vischer and French theologian Daniel Lys by way of footnotes in Jacques Ellul's inspiring books. Vischer had written a three-volume work entitled *The Witness of the Old Testament to Christ*, of which only volume 1 is translated into English.[2]

1. Then the Église réformée de France.
2. Wilhelm Vischer, *The Witness of the Old Testament to Christ*, vol. 1, *The*

That book, along with a number of articles and Daniel Lys' brilliant *The Meaning of the Old Testament*,[3] exposed us to a community of Bible scholars who articulated a continuity between the Old and New Testaments that was highly relevant then and now. This connection would ultimately lead me to Bourguet.

We experienced firsthand how a literal reading of the Old Testament in isolation from the New Testament confession that Jesus is both Lord and Christ (Messiah) brings great confusion, division, and even destruction. In rural Honduras churches often distinguish themselves by selective observance of Old Testament laws and use certain Old Testament stories to inspire fear of God as punishing judge. In North America Christians were drawing from the Old Testament to justify the death penalty and US military intervention in Central America and beyond.

Wilhelm Vischer himself had been an active resister of Nazism from his Old Testament teaching post inside Germany. He resisted the misuse of Scripture to justify anti-Semitism, nationalism, and war, insisting on the importance of the Old Testament for Christian faith at a time when it was being dismissed. He was consequently one of the first professors of theology to be pressured to leave his post and eventually depart Nazi Germany before World War II, and served as Karl Barth's pastor in Basel after he too left Germany. After the war, the church in France, having been widely engaged in resistance to Nazism and deeply encouraged by Barth, invited Vischer to be the professor of Old Testament at the IPT in Montpellier.

Ellul, Vischer, Lys and other French theologians were offering deep biblical reflection that led us to look into theological study in France.[4] We wrote the IPT about their graduate program and discov-

---

Pentateuch, trans. A. B. Crabtree (London: Lutterworth, 1949).

3. Daniel Lys, *The Meaning of the Old Testament* (Nashville: Abingdon, 1967).

4. We were able to study with pastor and New Testament professor Michel Bouttier, who was also trained by Vischer and published broadly, including a commentary on Ephesians and a number of collections of provocative articles. Elian Cuvillier followed Michel Bouttier and is currently Professor of New Testament at

ered that Vischer had long since retired after training several generations of pastors. His protégée, Daniel Lys, had recently retired but was still available. In Lys' place was his doctoral student Daniel Bourguet, who also had been trained by Vischer. The IPT welcomed us with a generous scholarship and we were soon making plans to learn French and move to Montpellier.

We were eager for help to understand Scripture after being immersed in Bible studies with impoverished farmers in war-torn Honduras. Disillusioned with America after being engaged in resisting US policy in Central America, we felt drawn to reflect from a different context. We reasoned that studying in a Protestant seminary with a history of persecution in a majority Catholic context would prove valuable. We left Tierra Nueva in the hands of local Honduran leaders and moved to Montpellier two months early to study French and began classes in September 1988.

Daniel Bourguet taught us Hebrew and Old Testament in ways that made the language and text come alive. He invited students into his passion and curiosity as we pondered both familiar and difficult passages of Scripture. I remember continually being surprised at how seriously Daniel took every textual critical variant, even seemingly irrelevant ones. He masterfully invited and guided us to both scrutinize and contemplate each variant in its original language until we understood the angle from which ancient interpreters had viewed the text. Daniel modeled an honoring of distinct perspectives as we studied the history of interpretation of each passage. He sought to hold diverse perspectives together whenever possible, yet only embraced what the text actually permitted, exemplifying fine-tuned discernment that inspired us.

Daniel's thorough approach meant he would only take us through a chapter or two per semester. This meant we took entire courses on Genesis 1-2:4, on Abraham's call in Genesis 12:1-4, and on Jeremiah 31, Exodus 1-2, Psalms 1-2 and others. In each of his courses he

---

the IPT, writing many high quality books and articles.

included relevant rabbinic exegesis, New Testament use of the Old Testament, and the church fathers' interpretations. Daniel imparted his confidence that God speaks good news now as he accompanied us in our reading, making our hearts burn like those of the disciples on the road to Emmaus—and inspiring us to want to do this with others. In alignment with Vischer and Lys he demonstrated through detailed exegesis of Old Testament texts how God's most total revelation in Jesus both fulfills and explains these Scriptures, making them come alive through the Holy Spirit in our lives and diverse contexts.

While living in France every summer Gracie and I traveled from France to Honduras, spending several weeks sharing our learning with Tierra Nueva's Honduran leadership and leading Bible studies in rural villages before returning back for classes in the Fall. We had pursued studies in France with the vision of bringing the best scholarship to the service of the least in a deliberate effort to bridge the divide between the academy and the poor. Our experience of the rare blend of scholarship and pastoral sensitivity, which you will see for yourself in his books, contributed to us feeling called back to the church, into ordained ministry and back to the United States to teach and minister there. I benefited from his being my dissertation supervisor as I continued to integrate regular study into our ministry of accompanying immigrants and inmates as we launched Tierra Nueva in Washington State.

Daniel Bourguet's writings are like high-quality wine extracted from vineyards planted in challenged soil. Born in 1946 in Aumessas, a small village in the Cévennes region of France, Daniel Bourguet grew up in the heartland of Huguenot Protestantism, which issued from the Reformation in the sixteenth century. He pursued studies of theology at the IPT in Montpellier, including study in Germany, Switzerland and at the Ecole Biblique in Jerusalem. In lieu of military service, Daniel served as a teacher in Madagascar. He was ordained as a pastor in the Église réformée de France in 1972, serving parishes from 1973 to 1987. Daniel wrote his doctoral dissertation[5] while serving as

5. See Daniel Bourguet, *Des métaphores de Jérémie*, Paris : J. Gabalda, 1987.

FOREWORD

a full-time parish pastor—a common practice in minority Protestant France, where teaching positions are scarce and pastors are in high demand. This practice often proves fruitful for ordinary Christians and theologians alike, deepening reflection and anchoring theologians in the church and world.

During our residential studies in Montpellier from 1988 to 1991, Gracie and I witnessed Daniel's interest in the early monastics and fathers of the Eastern church. In 1991 Daniel became prior of La Fraternité Spirituelle des Veilleurs (Spiritual Fraternity of the Watchpersons) and felt called to be a full-time monk, leaving the IPT in 1995 for a year in a Cistercian monastery in Lyon before moving to his current site in Les Cévennes in 1996.

Joy, simplicity, and mercy are the three pillars of Les Veilleurs, an association of laypeople and pastors founded by French Reformed pastor Wilfred Monod in 1923 (with a Francophone membership of four hundred in 2013). Members of this fellowship commit to pursuing daily rhythms of prayer and Scripture reading, including noontime recitation of the Beatitudes, Friday meditation on the cross, regular engagement with a faith community on Sundays, and spiritual retreats and reading that benefits from universal devotional and monastic practices. Les Veilleurs has served to nourish renewal in France and influenced the founding of communities such as Taizé. Under Daniel Bourguet's leadership Les Veilleurs thrived. As a member of Les Veilleurs I attended many of his annual retreats, witnessing and experiencing the vitality of this movement firsthand.

Daniel Bourguet's teaching and writing since his departure from his professorship at the IPT in 1995 have focused primarily on equipping ordinary Christians to grow spiritually through engaging in devotional practices such as prayer, Scripture reading and contemplation. Other works that will hopefully appear in English include reflections on asceticism, silence, daily prayer and the trinity. All but three of Daniel's twenty-five or so books are based on his spiritual retreats offered to pastors and retreatants with Les Veilleurs. He has offered retreats to

Foreword

Roman Catholic, Orthodox, and Protestant communities throughout France and Francophone Europe and is widely read and appreciated as a theologian who bridges divergent worlds and nourishes faithful Christian practice in France. Daniel Bourguet made his first and only visit to the United States in 2005, offering a spiritual retreat in Washington State. He accompanied me to Honduras on that same trip just after Hurricane Katrina ravaged the country, teaching Tierra Nueva's leaders and accompanying me as I led Bible studies and ministered in rural communities.

Daniel left his role as prior in 2012 and now continues his daily offices, receives many seekers for personal retreats, and offers occasional retreats where he lives and writes. In alignment with the early monastic commitment to manual labor, Daniel weaves black and white wool tapestries of illustrations of Biblical stories done by pastor and painter Henri Lindegaard. Daniel's unique contribution includes his Trinitarian approach to biblical interpretation wherein he reads Scripture informed by the early church fathers, with special sensitivity to how texts bear witness directly but also indirectly to Jesus, the Father and the Holy Spirit.

Daniel Bourguet models an approach to Scripture and spirituality desperately needed in our times. He reads the Bible with great confidence in God's goodness, discovering through careful reading, prayer, and contemplation insights that feed faith and inspire practice. Daniel's deliberate reading in communion with the church fathers brings the wisdom of the ages to nourish the body of Christ today. His tender love for people who come to him for spiritual support, and the larger church and world inform every page of his writing, inspiring like practice. May you find in this book refreshment, strength, and inspiration for your journey as you are drawn into deeper encounters with God.

Bob Ekblad

Mount Vernon, WA
July 7, 2016

Preface

THIS BOOK REPRISES STUDIES given during the year 2002 in the form of retreats of the Fraternité Sprituelle des Veilleurs, and on other similar occasions as at Crêt Berard (Switzerland) and the Abbey of Cîteaux, and again to a group of visitors to the hospital of Alès. In retreats, as with preaching, bibliographic references are left to one side; they might have had a place in marginal notes, but I have preferred to keep them to a minimum in order to stay close to the style of a retreat, as if the reader had also been invited to take part in a retreat through this book.

The people present at these retreats were believers, Christians, and the reader will see that my remarks assume this. Nothing has been changed here, so a reader who is not a believer will undoubtedly feel uncomfortable at times; for the host of questions that will arise for such a reader I ask pardon; however, to go on a retreat is to retire from the world for a time to be face to face with God and the teaching at a retreat is a means to that encounter; for this, a person would have to be a believer. You need to know this before starting to read the book; I am speaking here as if at a retreat, to a reader who is a believer.

Finally, again as if on a retreat, I have kept the elements of an oral style. You are addressed here as a "reader friend," in the form of a dialogue, a dialogue that doesn't propose to be more than an overture to the most sublime of dialogues, that with God.

So there we are, my reader friend! May your dialogue with God find something here to nourish it.

— CHAPTER 1 —

Christ and the Thief

32 Two others, malefactors, were led out to be executed with him. 33 When they arrived at the place known as The Place of the Skull, there they crucified him, together with the malefactors, one on his right, the other on his left. 34 Jesus said, "Father, forgive them, they know not what they do."

They parted his garments among themselves by the casting of lots. 35 The people stood there and looked on. The rulers mocked, saying, "He saved others, let him save himself if he is the Christ, the chosen."

36 The soldiers derided him, going up to him and giving him vinegar, 37 saying, "If you are the King of the Jews, save yourself." 38 There was an inscription above him, "This is the King of the Jews."

39 One of the crucified malefactors began to curse, saying, "Aren't you the Christ? Save yourself and us too." 40 But the other replied, rebuking him, "Have you no fear of God, you who are under the same condemnation as him? 41 For us this is justice, we are receiving our due reward, but he has done nothing wrong." Then he said, "Jesus, remember me when you come into your kingdom." Jesus said to him, "I tell you the truth, today you will be with me in paradise."

44 It was already about midday and there was darkness right across the entire land for three hours; 45 the sun had disappeared. The veil of the temple was split in two. 46 Then Jesus cried out in a loud voice, "Father, into thy hands I commit my spirit." Having said this, he breathed his last.

From Darkness to Light

> 47 Seeing what had happened, the centurion glorified God, saying, "Certainly, this was a just man." 48 All those who were present in the crowd, seeing events unfold, turned away, beating their breasts.
>
> 49. Those who knew him stood at a distance, as well as the women who had followed him from Galilee and were watching everything. (Luke 23)

No death, assuredly, can leave us indifferent; here, we have three men to watch as death approaches, three tortured men sharing their final moments side by side; among the three we find our Lord Jesus, the well-beloved Son of God the Father. Surely no other Bible passage is as poignant as this.

What Luke relates fills us with emotion, but an emotion so great that it is beyond understanding, beyond anything words can express. Luke, moreover, either doesn't know how or doesn't dare fully state it; for sure, it is in the silence that we can best seek to understand. Of silence, there is plenty; the text is full of it, overflowing, a fact that is easily recognized since what is described in these few lines constitutes the events of six hours. Six long hours of agony in just a dozen verses; this tells us the degree to which the account is pregnant with silence.

In the briefest of surveys of the text we can take in everything spoken by the men on the crosses; three times Jesus speaks, one of the criminals speaks once and the other twice. Six sentences in six hours! We see how deeply the agony of the three is marked by silence. Other comments are added to those of the condemned men, but these can be counted on the fingers of one hand; there are those of the rulers, the soldiers, and then, later, after Jesus' death, that of the centurion. That is all; everything else is silence ... Apart from the rulers and the soldiers, not a word is spoken by the people. Towards the back, somewhat apart, are a few of Jesus' friends with some women from Galilee, but neither do they break the silence. Death draws near without any sound, while, crowning everything, hovering over the scene, is the immense silence of God, to which no one could be indifferent . . . The Son dies enfolded in the silence of his Father.

When the sun disappears, this does the reverse of breaching the silence which reigns. The darkness steals, noiselessly, across the entire land. One sound alone comes to disturb the silence, a most strange, even anguished sound, that of the veil of the temple being ripped . . . After this rending sound, the silence takes hold again, so deeply that it is possible to hear Jesus' final breath.

And so Jesus dies. It is our turn to be seized with silence, faced with the inexpressible.

Six long hours

Luke gives just one piece of information about the timespan of these events; he tells us that the darkness filled the land for three hours, from midday until three (v. 44). Because of Mark we can say that Jesus' agony stretched across about six hours, since he tells us that the tortured men were crucified at nine in the morning (15:25).

According to John's Gospel, we know that Jesus was dead before the other two unfortunates (19:32–33), without our knowing exactly how long the pain of these two continued. It was however no more than a few hours, since their legs were broken so they would die more quickly, before the onset of night.

Such is this account, both extraordinarily sober and dense; we need to meditate it slowly, to the rhythm of the words and silences, knowing that its depth is too great for us.

Companionship in death

In this account we are going to pay careful attention to the companionship of the dying men. Seen from this angle, the account is once again extraordinary. We are presented with the agony of two criminals who have the immense privilege of being accompanied in their deaths by none other than Jesus himself. Jesus will wonderfully be right alongside the two men, and goes so far as to share their death and die with them. Who would not long to have Jesus alongside them in this way?

At the same time, while Jesus accompanies the two dying men by dying with them, he himself has the company in death of the same two tortured companions. Jesus does not die alone; his two neighbors also share his death. Certainly each of them accompanies Jesus in his own way, one of them cursing, the other being converted, but they are indeed there, and we find that Jesus, for better or for worse, was afforded their company; neither should we forget the companionship of all those others who were witnesses of his death. They too were there with contrasting attitudes, the sarcasm of some, but also the moving silence of others, which we feel to have been compassionate on the part of those who knew him; this was surely the case with the women from Galilee, whose eyes never left him through the long hours of agony; a comforting presence, to which we should add that of the centurion, whose final exclamation denotes his rapt attention.

Such is the text which enables us to contemplate Jesus alongside the two dying men as he died with them, accompanied by them in his agony.

An exchange of words and silences

To die at Jesus' side; is this not extraordinary? It is so much so that Luke invites us in his account to participate in this as a mystery, and yet he is the only Gospel writer to do so! Might this be because as a doctor

Luke feels closer to the dying? Perhaps. It's certainly the case that the other three evangelists, together in agreement as to mentioning the presence of the two crucified criminals, say nothing of their encounter with Christ. Luke is alone in reporting the few words that passed between the three tortured men; it is him we follow as we engage with the dialogue.

A six-hour dialogue is a lengthy one! Certainly, according to the Gospels, it is the longest of any in which Jesus participated. An exchange with so few words and so much silence is also very unusual; indeed it is so exceptional that the silences of the account cannot be neglected; they are as much to be explored as the words. The fact is that in this encounter each silence throws into relief and prolongs the impact of the speech; in short, the words and silences alongside each other interpenetrate and mingle, there for our meditation.

The source for Luke's account

Luke was not one of the first generation disciples, but had to rely on a multitude of witnesses in preparing his Gospel (see 1:2). Who then was it who heard the dialogue between Jesus and the thief, and then told it to Luke? Who was close enough to the cross to have heard what the crucified men were saying? Who had Luke been able to interview so as to report what none of the other evangelists do?

Matthew and Mark only report the words of Jesus from the cross that were cried out in a loud voice, as is specified in their two Gospels (Matt 27:46, 50; Mark 15:34, 37). They record only Jesus' cries; the accounts they provide us are those of witnesses who stood at a distance. In John, things are different, but this is easily understood, because this disciple stood near the cross. As for Luke, he most certainly was not at the foot of the cross to hear what he has nevertheless passed on to us. Who was his informant?

Near the cross, Luke tells us, there also stood some women. Which of these did he speak to if not the same person he interviewed with regard to Jesus childhood, that is, Mary, Jesus' mother? The whole account of Jesus childhood manifestly has its origin in the information given by Mary. The crucifixion account must, it seems to me, come from the same source.

Mary, John tells us, was also near the cross (John 19:25), but curiously Luke is silent on this point; one wonders why. Luke surely knew from Mary herself that she had stood near the cross, so why does he say nothing of this? The silence conveys, I believe, Luke's sensitivity towards Mary's suffering. At the foot of the cross this mother's pain is beyond anything, inexpressible. Luke is so unable to put this extreme pain into words that he prefers to keep silent, though the silence is not total.

At the beginning of his Gospel, Luke reports the prophecy given in the temple by Simeon to Mary. Filled with the Holy Spirit, the old man had announced, "And you yourself shall be pierced through to the soul with a sword" (2:35). This was exactly the suffering of Mary at the foot of the cross, the suffering of a sword piercing the soul . . . something beyond understanding.

Near the cross, Mary knew the pain announced by Simeon. Luke knew this and tells us of it early in his Gospel; he does not repeat it, it is not restated.

If Mary was Luke's favored witness in his account of the crucifixion, then certain aspects of his account become clear.

The conversation Mary heard between her son and the good thief must have been a tremendous solace to her sorrowful heart. In the midst of all the insults, she had the joy of hearing a man speak to her son with gentleness; "Jesus, remember me when you come into your kingdom." Finally, someone who was not attacking him. What a great relief for Mary, who could surely not forget such words.

What a further release for her to then hear the no less unforgettable reply, "You will be with me today in paradise." What a comfort for this mother! Her son will be in paradise! Today even . . . The soul, pierced through by a sword, receives from her son a means to live and not die of sorrow.

Mary could give herself over to what she had heard, even when darkness was invading the land. Through the dark hours, she is so enveloped in this word of hope that she scarcely hears what was nevertheless heard at a distance, which Matthew and Mark report, "My God, my God, why have you forsaken me?"

This cry of pain, which would be insupportable to a mother, passes Mary by! Her pierced soul is elsewhere, carried away by the evocation of paradise.

The whole of the account of the cross in Luke comes from Mary, who tells only what she had been able to grasp with her pierced but then quieted soul. This imprints the account with a paradoxical sweetness that is not found in the other evangelists. Through Luke we hear a mother tell of her son's death . . . Jesus never cries out; he only breaks his silence to fill a thief with hope. As to the rest, he is engaged solely in prayer, turning entirely towards his Father, as he had always done (cf. Luke 2:49).

The suffering on the cross

There is another point that can be explained by the fact that Luke's account comes from Mary; nothing is said of what the physical suffering endured by Jesus on the cross would have been. Luke is silent on this point while earlier in his Gospel he records the actual words of Jesus announcing that he would "suffer greatly" (9:22; see also 22:15 and 24:26, 46).

We understand; like any mother, Mary was perforce most sensitive to the sufferings undergone by her son, but it was impossible to speak of them. A mother cannot find words to say what for her is unbearable.

The first words

When the three condemned men had been nailed to their individual instruments of torture, the first to speak was Jesus. No one else from among the torturers, the friends, the onlookers, speaks. Golgotha is in silence around the three crucified men; they, therefore, have the opportunity to speak; they are close enough to one another and still physically able.

Jesus is the first to speak, and from the outset his words could only invite and indeed require silence. He doesn't speak to his crucified fellows nor to anyone in the crowd. They are nevertheless spoken aloud, with enough strength that the other two would at least hear. These first words are a prayer: "Father, forgive them, they know not what they do."

Neither of the two criminals reacts at this moment to the prayer, but it makes its way into the heart of each, into each one's silence, as we become aware in the rest of the passage.

The one who should have replied to Jesus' words would be the one to whom they were addressed: God . . . But God is silent! The silence around Golgotha after Jesus' prayer underscores God's silence. Will God respond? As this response is awaited, God's silence invites each person to be silent too; it provides space for each one to ponder and for this prayer of Jesus to penetrate more deeply.

We may not know the pathway Jesus' prayer took in the heart of all those who heard it, but we can be sure that one of the two malefactors was very moved by it, and that from that basis it runs an entire course that leads to nothing less extraordinary than conversion.

Not only is Jesus accompanying the two men in dying, but he is accompanying one of them along the road of conversion; the way he does this is indeed out of the ordinary.

An unnoticed conversion

The two tortured men are no better than "bandits," as we are told by Matthew (27:38, 44) and Mark (15:27); "malefactors" according to Luke; in short, less than entirely respectable people! For greater clarity, to distinguish between the two malefactors I will refer to the one who is converted as "the good thief," following tradition, but without this intending any judgment on the other.

On a cross, as with any place of torture, the chances are high of meeting people who keep bad company! This is certainly the case with regard to Jesus' neighbors, but Jesus had no choice. However, he shows no distaste for them; on the contrary! Throughout his ministry he never ceased to say that he had come for the sinners, and here he is now between two of them. They gave him an opportunity to continue his ministry, and that is what, in fact, he does. Wonderful Jesus, who until his final breath accomplishes the task committed to him.

Is it because the two were brigands that Mark, Matthew, and John pay no attention to the dialogue between the crucified men? I don't know, but it is possible. We do need to note that in passing it over in silence they miss out the conversion, which has so much to say to us.

Here is a brigand who is converted at the hour of his death. This should cause us to reflect on the death of less respectable folk, even notorious pagans. Here is a man on his way to paradise when all the world would consign him to hell. Here is a man who dies sanctified by a word from Jesus, but upon whom Matthew, Mark, and John bestow no attention. We must not judge outsiders, the less respectable, even notorious thieves . . . Who knows what may happen at the moment of their death. The good thief's conversion shows us that hearts may, altogether unknown to us, open up to faith. Eyes may be opened to the consideration of Christ at the moment of death.

No disciple had been at any pains to evangelize these two malefactors; no one had prayed for them as their deaths approached. Only

Jesus cares, as a shepherd cares for each of his sheep, even the sheep that is lost. Blessed Jesus!

In God's presence

Jesus' first words are a prayer. Luke reports this, in v. 34, immediately after twice mentioning the presence of the two malefactors (vv. 32 and 33), clearly indicating that they heard the prayer, even if it was not addressed directly to them. Jesus might have prayed in a low voice or in his heart, but he didn't. This must mean that he made sure of being heard by his two companions in pain.

Rather than speak directly to the two malefactors, Jesus prefers to pray before them, making them aware of a presence of which they had perhaps no suspicion, that of God. If Jesus addresses himself to God it is because he is truly there. Jesus speaks to him as he would speak to the thieves, with the same intensity of voice. This is the first teaching Jesus drops into the hearts of his companions in death: when death approaches, it is good to pray. A first teaching and perhaps a first shock too, since the malefactors were perhaps little inclined to prayer! Perhaps, indeed, this was the first time for them to hear anyone pray alongside them. Here, in their agony, someone is opening before them the pathway of prayer, in the silence of God.

These two criminals have no idea of their privilege; few indeed are those who had heard Jesus pray. In Gethsemane, Jesus had asked his disciples to keep company with him in prayer, and all had slept! Here are two malefactors, and they are alongside Jesus as he prays; blessed malefactors! One of them will set to cursing, but the other will follow Jesus along the way of prayer, so well indeed that he will turn towards him to address to him his very first prayer, "Jesus, remember me when you come into your kingdom."

In the presence of the Father

To die praying, this is Jesus' first teaching as he accompanies these two. However, the way he prays and the content of his prayer completes the teaching: "Father, forgive them, they know not what they do."

"Father!" Jesus says. But who in fact is he addressing when he speaks this way? It is well known that in their last moments dying men often speak to those who have gone before, as if to throw a bridge across the gulf between the living and the dead. Many people in the throes of death call out for their father or their mother or some other intimate who has already died. Perhaps Jesus is doing the same? Some of those who were at Golgotha thought so, if we follow the other evangelists, who report that when they heard Jesus cry "Eli!" (which is to say, "my God," in Aramaic), some believed that Jesus was calling on the prophet Elijah, who had departed a long time since (Matt 27:46–49).

After all, if some people believed that Jesus called on Elijah, others might have thought that by saying "father," Jesus was invoking Joseph of Nazareth. However, Luke leaves no room for this type of confusion, and the malefactors themselves made no such mistake. The good thief, certainly, was quite clear that Jesus was addressing God, which is why he began to speak to the other of God, saying to him, "Don't you fear God?" The thought of God came to him as a result of Jesus' prayer on the cross.

The Father and the Son

"Father," Jesus then says, addressing God, without having to cry out, without speaking more loudly than when speaking to the good thief. Is God that close? Might he be as close as the crucified men are to each other? The malefactors know nothing of this, but they discover what for Jesus is a reality, that God is close even if he is silent. This discovery has in it further matter to plunge the good thief into silence.

"Father," he says from the cross. If the two malefactors had perhaps not often heard anyone pray, they had certainly never heard anyone speak to God in this way. It was not at all the custom in Israel to pray to God calling him "Father." Furthermore, implicit in this innovation is that Jesus considers himself the Son of the one he prays to. Such a relationship with God has plenty to maintain the thief's silence.

"Father": the vocative is a word that, in Jesus' mouth, is always particularly charged with love. The malefactors were perhaps not prepared to hear, on this instrument of torture, a word of love spoken to God! Obviously they would be silent after what Jesus has just said. They have plenty to think about deeply.

"Father": the Greek word used by Luke is very surely a translation of what Jesus must have said in Aramaic, as Mark teaches us (14:36) when he tells us at the same point that the Greek word translates Jesus' Aramaic; this was much more emotionally charged than the Greek because in Aramaic "Abba" corresponds more closely to "Dad" than "Father"; the Greek lacks such nuances.

For the thief, this "Dad" addressed to God by Jesus has the effect of rendering him still more deeply silent. Plenty of people speak after Jesus—the rulers, the soldiers, the other thief . . . the good thief is the one who is silent the longest. We understand; there was so much to consider with this "Dad," for which he was so little prepared.

On the cross the good thief discovers both the Father and the Son . . . He is inducted into an infinite mystery and it fills his silence!

An inexpressible love

The good thief seems to sense the inexpressible love that unites the Father and the Son. To discover this he has nothing but the short prayer spoken at his side, followed by the very lengthy silence Jesus himself observes; this becomes part of his own silence and little by little illuminates it. After this long silence, when the thief finally speaks, he dares not pronounce the word "love," but speaks only of "fear" to his crucified fellow: "Don't you fear God?" When he says this, no doubt it is because he himself is aware of this feeling he calls "fear," a feeling that is unknown to him and had not prevented him from becoming a criminal, a feeling that he has just discovered in listening to Jesus' prayer and that he is astonished not to find in his fellow. "Don't you fear God?" with its implicit, "as for me, I fear him now!"

This fear of God is respect, not terror. In the Bible, fear is the nascent love that one can have for God; it is the prelude to a love full of respect, but in which affection has as yet no place. "Abba," says something else, a great love in which affection has chased away fear. In speaking only of the "fear of God," the thief is gauging the distance there is between what he feels and the feeling of the one who has just said "Dad!"

"Father," "Abba": with what intonation did Jesus say the word? It would be so important to know! Intonation, tone of voice, is indeed of great importance, but it's not something Luke is able to transmit. Blessed thief who heard, and whose heart it left silently impregnated.

An open love for others

"Father": at the hour of death it is common to cling to God, for reassurance, to find in him the peace and strength necessary to forge this formidable passage; in such a case prayer is a cry for help, but Jesus' prayer has none of this. From the cross there is nothing he requests for himself; he is not focused on himself but on others. Jesus' love for his Father is not to be kept to himself but is totally open to others. In love, Christ humbly effaces himself and places others between his Father and himself: "Father, forgive them, for they know not what they do."

The most spiritually minded tell us that the closer one is to God the more attentive one is to others. The thief must have felt this in Jesus' prayer. He had never met a man so close to God. In his silence, the thief slowly discovers the Father and the Son; Jesus asks nothing for himself, all his desire of the Father is for others.

Pardon for a wrong

"Forgive them": who is designated by the pronoun "them"? Of whom exactly is Jesus speaking? Most certainly, of those responsible for the crucifixion, of all those who had led him out to the cross. Jesus prays for the anonymous, undefined "them" of whom Luke speaks in his account, "*they* arrived at the place called the Skull and there *they* crucified him." This is indeed the case, but while this is so, the malefactors are not incidental to the crucifixion; they are undergoing it with him, but it is not for them that Jesus is praying. For this reason the thief might feel himself to be outside of Jesus' prayer. He is not concerned in it; his part is silence.

"Forgive them," but forgive what? The death sentence? No doubt! But if the sentence is just and is a just application of the law, then there can be no need of forgiveness. Forgiveness is not for what is right; pardon applies only where there is injustice. Had there been injustice in Jesus' condemnation? Of course, and this is what the thief must think and why he says to the other malefactor: "In our case it is just that we are condemned, but he has done nothing wrong." This is surely how things stand; unjust condemnation explains why Jesus can speak of pardon. As for the good thief, he recognizes that he is not the victim of injustice; he is no position to identify with Jesus' prayer.

Neither responsible for Jesus' death, nor the victim like Jesus of an injustice, the good thief decidedly has reason to feel uninvolved in the prayer of his neighbor; it does not concern him. He has no reason to intrude on what Jesus says to his Father.

If there is injustice in Jesus' case then it touches Jesus firstly and it is for him to forgive. If now Jesus asks his Father to forgive it must be because the injustice also touches him. To clearly understand Jesus, he is saying that the injustice done the Son affects the Father just as much; Jesus and God are victims of men together! The thief is silent before the communion he discovers between the Father and the Son; their fellowship of love is also a fellowship of suffering; while the Son is wounded in his body, the Father is wounded in his heart: "Father, forgive them, because they don't know the evil they are doing to You in putting me to death."

The thief discovers that the Father can suffer, that God can suffer! He truly has reason to be sunk in silence . . . To have asked what he does, the Son must know the Father's suffering, but in this prayer it is left as an implication; he says no more out of sensitive concern for a wounded heart; it is the sensitivity of great intimacy.

After Jesus' prayer, the Father does not reply to the Son, but is silent and says nothing in his sorrow. His response is quiet reticence. The Father and the Son are united in the silence of intimacy.

"Forgive them": everyone else who speaks after Jesus at Golgotha sees things quite differently; no one, in fact, speaks of forgiveness. They all coincide in another notion, another demand: "Let him *save* himself," say the rulers; "*Save* yourself," add the soldiers (v. 37); and the other malefactor repeats as if an echo, "*Save* yourself" (v. 39). They all speak of salvation and do so in mockery! Jesus is alone in speaking of pardon, without a hint of mockery. The disaccord is total . . . The good thief has reason to be silent before sizing things up and eventually taking his stand.

"To save oneself" in the present case would be to escape the consequences of others' actions and from death. "To forgive," is something else again; it is to bear with the actions of others and supersede them, purifying them of all wrong. It is not to escape death, but to accept it and transcend it.

The love that pardons

When Jesus asks his Father to forgive, it implies that he himself has already done so. Effectively, had he not already forgiven, he wouldn't be asking the same of God. Thus, the thief finds that alongside him is a victim of injustice who has forgiven and asks God to forgive too. When a victim and God agree together in forgiving, the forgiveness is full and complete. Such is Jesus' longing for this crowd of guilty people—total forgiveness. Surely this crucified man must overflow with love to pray in this way.

"They don't know what they do," says Jesus. If they don't know, they can't ask for pardon. Thus, Jesus is asking of God forgiveness which the guilty parties cannot ask for themselves; Jesus asks in their place. This also means that he has forgiven without his forgiveness being asked. What love, and what humility too, since it surely requires humility to forgive before forgiveness has been asked. In silence the thief becomes aware of what is transpiring in Jesus heart in the course of his brief prayer: his love, his humility.

"Father, forgive them": Jesus speaks of forgiveness to God, not to the crowd. At no point, moreover, does he say anything to the crowd during the long hours of agony. This is strange! It would be easy for him to harangue the people from up on the cross, to say who knows what while he still had strength; he could declaim his innocence before all; he could convince of their error those who clamored for his death; he could announce his forgiveness; and since he is full of love, he could preach a sermon on love . . . But Jesus does none of this. He doesn't preach on love or anything else from the cross; he has no wish to persuade . . . he prays and that is all. He doesn't preach love, he lives it through his intercession and in acceptance of the death he suffers on others' behalf.

There is so much love in Jesus, and it is for the guilty! He doesn't pray for the silent women standing at a distance who are in no way guilty of this injustice; on the contrary, he prays for those who called for his death, for his assassins. If the thief never heard the sermon Jesus had pronounced one day on a hillside in Galilee, inviting loving prayer for one's enemies, he nevertheless now sees this love lived out on the hill of Golgotha. This prayer says more to him than any sermon . . .

On the cross, Jesus carries all the people in his prayer as a shepherd carries a sheep that has strayed. This is the mission entrusted him by his Father; he fulfils it until his final breath.

"They know not what they do"

In the sequel to his Gospel, the book of Acts, Luke makes a commentary of sorts on this phrase. The people and their leaders believed they were doing well in having Jesus condemned. They thought it was right to have him crucified, thinking his punishment was a just application of the Law. But the apostle Peter states that it was not so much a judicial condemnation as simply an assassination; "You killed him," he says crudely (Acts 3:15). Then, the apostle adds, "I know that you did it in ignorance, as did your rulers" (3:17). These people, guilty "in ignorance," no doubt had a good conscience. They believed they were pleasing God in ridding the world of a blasphemer who made himself equal with God in presenting himself as his Son. They believed they were doing good, protecting society from a smooth talker who was likely to unleash Roman repression. Good intentions are generally accompanied by a good conscience!

What a chasm between a good conscience and God! What a chasm when we don't know the ill we do to God. Jesus crosses this chasm in asking of God our pardon, in forgiving our good conscience, our good intentions, our illusions, our blindness! How blessed we are to receive of the Father and the Son their forgiveness.

Today, when we encounter someone at fault through ignorance, we make efforts to remove the fault, shifting the blame onto others, but the Old Testament no more does this than the New. Peter confirms the guilt of ignorance (Acts 3:17); he reveals it, puts it forward as an invitation to repentance and to then plead for forgiveness (3:19). An ignorant wrongdoer is just as much a wrongdoer! On the cross Jesus does not seek to minimize the guilt of anyone: he asks for God's forgiveness.

To go the way of denying guilt is another way of attempting to save oneself, to do without God. To deny blame and not to feel one's guilt will not bring God's intervention. Pardon cannot pass out of God's hands because God alone can pardon in truth, as the Old Testament tells us by making God the sole subject of the Hebrew verb "forgive" (*sālah*). Even among men, forgiveness lacks real force when it is not supported by, accompanied by, the forgiveness of God. Even Jesus, as he forgives his torturers, asks his Father to add his forgiveness to his own. A merely human pardon is not deep enough to be fully functional.

In the thief's silence

In silence, the thief discovers at his side a man who forgives the irresponsible, and who asks of God support for this forgiveness.

This, in short, is the summation of what the good thief discovers on the road towards conversion during the hours of silence which follow Jesus' prayer. Does he still feel outside the scope of the prayer, as one who has no guilt in Jesus' death? It may be that this malefactor has made a review of his life in the light of the prayer and found there all the evil he might have unknowingly done in the course of his life . . . and yet this would be as nothing beside the known! If Luke refers to the man as a "malefactor," it is not without reason. If he finds himself nailed to an instrument of torture, it is surely because he had committed evil acts, no doubt more knowingly than otherwise, and so, on this point too, the malefactor could not but feel at the margin of Jesus' prayer. In effect, Jesus had prayed for the unknown faults of his torturers and not for deliberate ills. What, then, was to become of the malefactor and all his deliberate misdeeds? The thief will finish by posing Jesus a question: you who care for all the irresponsible and pray for them, you who love them to the point of seeking their pardon, what will you make of those who know they have done wrong? What will you make of a bad man who knows himself to be responsible for a sea of faults? "Jesus, remember me when you come into your kingdom."

The work of the Holy Spirit

Before we follow further the pathway to conversion followed by this malefactor, we should dwell a little on the fact that one of the two takes the path of conversion while the other blasphemes, though both had heard the same prayer! How is it that one is touched by Christ's prayer and the other is not? That one enters the intimate communion of the love of the Father and the Son while the other does not?

This assuredly comes from the Holy Spirit and no one else. No one other than the Spirit can bring us into the intimacy of the Father and the Son, because, in God, this intimacy of Father and Son is shared with the Holy Spirit. The Spirit alone can introduce us into the trinitarian intimacy; we are dealing here with one of the depths of God which the Spirit alone can sound (1 Cor 2:10) and reveal to us. There is no pathway of conversion without the breath of the Holy Spirit . . . if the good thief is advancing along this path it is because the Holy Spirit has taken a hold of him, working in him, opening him up to the Father and the Son. It is through the Spirit that the thief can enter into the prayer the Son speaks to the Father.

With regard to the other malefactor, he is being driven along another route, that of blasphemy and curses . . . but where will this lead him? We know nothing. What will become of this blasphemer later? How will he take the reply which is addressed to him, the exchange between the good thief and Jesus, Jesus' final prayer, the centurion's exclamation . . . ? We know nothing because this malefactor retreats into silence. There is nothing to say whether his final silence was occupied with new blasphemies or with the Holy Spirit. This is a matter for God, who alone knows what was to become in the end of the thief who blasphemed . . .

Let us return to the good thief, whose conversion is reported by Luke. It is essential we understand that a malefactor can be converted at the hour of his death and to know that this is the work of the Holy Spirit in him. Indeed, the Holy Spirit is at work in the dying, and it is he moreover, rather than we, who truly accompanies them. We who draw alongside the dying must know that the Spirit accompanies each one and that this is a reality on which we can rely.

As he enters with the Spirit into the mystery of the Father and the Son, the good thief enters into the mystery of the Trinity, and, along with this, the mystery of prayer, of forgiveness, and of love. There is no more wonderful close to a life than that of this man. Thanks to, and through, the Spirit he understands what Jesus says and agrees with it.

When will Jesus proclaim his forgiveness?

The crowd of mockers and scorners could not understand Jesus' forgiveness, which is why Jesus does not speak to them. He knows that his forgiveness will not be received. It is not necessary to respond to these mockers and scorners; mockery comes from hearts closed to forgiveness.

When then will Jesus speak of his pardon to his torturers and to all of us who crucify him again in so many ways? I gladly believe that he will publish his forgiveness on the last day. Then all of us, his knowing or unknowing torturers, will see the lamb that was slain. He will have only to show us his wounds and his pierced side and that will be enough for us to measure the depth of our fault. He will be able to simply turn towards his Father and say to him, "Father, forgive them, because they didn't know what they were doing!" Then, in our silence and confusion, our closed hearts will open to forgiveness and the Father will fulfill his Son's desire . . .

The Father's gift to the Son

Without waiting until the final day for the revelation of full forgiveness, the Father will grant his Son's wish, at least partially, right here at the cross, by opening the heart of the good thief to this pardon. The good thief's conversion is the gift the Father presents the Son as a sign of acceptance. It is a wonderful miracle, full of an infinite love; in this thief the Father gives the Son a brother to die with him, by his side. The good thief is the consolation given to the Son at the hour of his death, just as Christ is the consolation given to the good thief.

The heart of a malefactor opens; a miracle accomplished by the Father in silence, humbly.

This humble and discreet miracle could not escape the attention of Jesus, Jesus who was possessed of this certainty, that "No one can come to me unless the Father draws him" (John 6:44). The thief comes to Christ; this is a work of God, a wonderful sign received by the Son from his Father.

Reader friend, for a long time I have wondered why Luke does not report Jesus' cry from the cross, "My God, my God, why have you forsaken me?" Where Matthew and Mark do report this cry, they say nothing of the good thief's conversion. It now seems to me that, for Luke, the good thief's conversion demonstrates to the Son that the Father has not abandoned him. Jesus dies without the slightest doubt on this matter, in great peace; "Father, into Thy hands I commit my spirit." This is why, too, Jesus can speak to the thief of paradise with complete certainty.

Waves of violence

Along the road to his conversion, the silent thief sees great waves of violence beat against Jesus, streams of verbal violence which mount up against him to a point of crescendo. Luke describes this crescendo very specifically.

The first to open their mouths against Christ are the rulers, who deride him. The word used for "deride" or "scorn" (its main meaning is to "expel air through the nostrils") expresses the derision of which Jesus was the object.

After this derision comes the more stinging mockery in the mouths of the soldiers. The verb chosen by Luke for "mock" means rather more precisely "to treat as a child"; this is frankly malicious as concerning a man who has just prayed to his Father. To treat as a child an adult who has just used the word "dad" is deeply wounding.

The third wave of violence proceeds from the other tortured man, who, as Luke puts it, "curses" or "blasphemes." The words of the malefactor are on the whole the same as those of the soldiers, which are described as mockery. Why then is the verb "blaspheme" the evangelist's choice? A blasphemy is an insult addressed to God. If the malefactor "blasphemes," as Luke says, it is because Jesus is here touched in his divinity, the deepest place in the mystery of his being. With the malefactor's blasphemy, the crescendo of violence reaches its peak.

This crescendo is accentuated by its increasing physical proximity to Jesus. Firstly, the derision comes from the rulers, who are at something of a distance from Jesus. Then from the soldiers, who are nearer the cross, since they are said to "come up to him," as specified by Luke. This proximity is still greater given that the soldiers don't restrict themselves to the third person used by the rulers ("let him save himself") but change to the second person, which necessarily touches Jesus more closely: "Save yourself." The final blasphemer is even closer, on the cross at his side; he also calls Jesus familiarly "you."

To this diversity of verbal violence are added actions whose violence is again overt. First, there is the parting of the dying man's garments, like a legacy of which possession is taken before the fellow is even dead. Then there is the vinegar, offered as one more mockery to a man athirst in his agony.

The good thief's intervention

This inundation of violence converges on Christ and on him alone. The thief has no concern in it; he is no more than a witness, as he is also, however, to the absence of any reaction by Jesus to this violence. What would he, the thief, have done, subjected to such violence? He would surely react by violence in turn, as would any self-respecting villain!

Seeing the absence of reaction on Jesus' part, the thief decides to intervene. He does so following the third wave of violence, that coming from the other malefactor. He reacts by taking up the defense of Jesus, this innocent man, accused by all the world but who does not defend himself. The cause of this reaction from the thief at this exact moment is seeing a fellow criminal join the chorus of the rulers and the soldiers. Among companions in being tortured there is respect; among crucified men, solidarity! There is to be a common front against the torturers! How could it be that a fellow would join himself to the thinking of the rulers and soldiers? Faced with this enormity, the good thief reacts and reprimands the traitor to make him shut up; but he does it in a way that goes beyond the simple expectation of solidarity among companions in pain.

"Don't you fear God, you who are suffering the same condemnation as him?" Who does the "him" in the thief's mouth refer to—Jesus or God? Everything the thief says applies as much to God as to Jesus. The fellowship between the Son and the Father is such that for the thief they are one. Indeed, what the malefactor has said is a real blasphemy against Jesus, against God, because this Jesus on the cross is the Son of God.

Just how far does the communion of love between Jesus and God extend, between the Father and the Son? The mystery is too great for the thief; but that doesn't mean he is unaware that it is far from ordinary.

The good thief does not perhaps know that the other fellow is quite simply being manipulated by the prince of darkness, who has taken hold of him, causing him to blaspheme as one possessed. The thief is unaware that Satan has drawn near the cross.

The hidden presence of Satan

At the close of the account of Jesus' temptation, Luke has a phrase which we do well to bear in mind: "After tempting him in all these ways, the devil withdrew *until a more favorable moment*" (4:13). These last words are formidable and require us to ask when the "favorable moment" would be that the devil would choose to approach Christ afresh. This attempt is not clearly identified by Luke in the ensuing chapters of his Gospel. If the attempt was not an open one, as it was in the desert, perhaps it took place by dissimulation, by a ruse or trickery. Everything leads one to believe that Satan drew near here at the cross, at the moment when Jesus is most vulnerable and at his weakest.

Luke effectively invites us to discern the hidden presence of Satan. The three waves of verbal violence look like a triple temptation aimed at having Jesus descend from the cross to save himself and so renounce his mission.

To help us spot the hidden presence of the tempter, Luke gives us a clear indication in the soldiers' choice of words: "If you are the King of the Jews."

When the devil drew near in the wilderness, his tactic was as follows: to put forward a statement that was true and slip an enticing suggestion in with it. Twice in this way he says, "If you are the Son of God" (4:3, 9), which contains a statement of truth, drawn from what God had said immediately before at the baptism; then Satan adds to this statement his tempting suggestions: change the rocks into bread, jump from the temple pinnacle. On the cross his procedure is the same: "If you are the King of the Jews," which affirms a truth drawn from the inscription fixed above Jesus which Luke records, "This is the King of the Jews" (23:38). Based on this statement of truth, Satan, in the mouth of the soldiers, makes his tempting suggestion, "If you are the King of the Jews, save yourself."

This then is clear; through the soldiers it is Satan who is speaking. Luke doesn't name him, to show that he hides himself, but he does everything else to make us aware of his presence. Jesus' prayer from the cross becomes still clearer. "Father, forgive them, for they know not what they do"; yes, Father, forgive the people, forgive the rulers, forgive the soldiers, all of them, because they don't know that they are being manipulated . . . Jesus does not name the puppeteer, his name is so despicable.

Faced with temptation

In the wilderness Jesus had responded to Satan when he stepped forward openly. Here on the cross Jesus does not respond to him as he now hides. Faced with the enemy's dissimulation, Jesus has just one riposte, prayer. Never forget, reader friend, when faced with the tempter, there is no better weapon than prayer. Don't measure off against someone more cunning than yourself. Base your attitude on that of Christ and pray. Turn to the Father, with the Son and in the Spirit, and let your only words be addressed to God.

In his non-response to the rulers, the soldiers, or the thief, who all attack him verbally, we can see that Jesus has no ill-feeling towards these people; rather, his attitude demonstrates a refusal to respond to the tempter. With regard to the people being used by Satan, Jesus cannot but carry them in his intercession, "Father, forgive them . . ."

The verbal violence to which Jesus is subjected on the cross is not just human violence; in it there is the violence of the adversary. For Jesus the cross is a time of arduous combat, infinitely beyond what we could cope with. Against each assault of the tempter, Jesus resists through prayer; it is prayer, and its contents are not reactive against the tempter's attack; it is not, "Father, save me," but, "Father, save them by forgiving them."

In this battle of unprecedented violence Jesus fights alone, but he has a surprising source of help, given him in a wonderful way by the Father. In Gethsemane, in his struggle against the enemy, he was given an angel to strengthen him (22:43). On the cross, it is not an angel who is given in this way, but the good thief. Unbeknownst to him, the good thief, in his conversion, is a gift from the Father to the Son to sustain him in the battle.

Satan has placed his hand on the rulers, on the soldiers, on one of the malefactors, and so advanced closer and closer, right up to the neighboring cross, but is unable to lay a hand on the good thief, who God preserves, filling him with a humble love for Christ; "Jesus, remember me . . ." Jesus makes no mistake here; he answers no one except the thief and speaks to him as a friend speaks to his friend: "I tell you the truth, today you will be with me in paradise."

Free or enslaved?

Faced with the unfurling of violence of which he is witness, no doubt without realizing its spiritual depth, the good thief would feel right at home, in the world of violence he knows well. All his life the thief had been marked by violence. On the cross, he could have joined the interplay of violence and yielded to it. Of course, he is impeded from physical violence, his nailed hands unable to strike, but his tongue is free, free to attack the entire world, including God should his heart so dictate. He could spit hatred to his final breath . . . but he does nothing of the sort. He knows only too well—death will have the last word. The death of a crucified man is the victory of those who condemn him; the thief's death will be the victory of others. He will be defeated, "executed," as Luke most accurately describes it (v. 32).

Death's victory, this is to be the final stage in the cycle of violence in which the thief has always lived, a cycle in which, in the end, he is not free, but a slave. His freedom to attack anything that might offer itself to him on the cross is an illusory freedom, a last kick of a long lost liberty. Death has the final word; this is the law of sin which leads to death, the law of Satan.

On the cross the thief is silent; he takes no part in the sport of violence, no doubt for the first time! The cause of this is his neighbor's prayer. His life is at a tipping point, led there by this man who in no way enters the round of aggression. This violent world is ignorant of the one essential thing that Christ comes to bring into prominence: forgiveness. If vengeance and hatred are the engine that feeds violence, the heart of Satan's logic, then forgiveness and love defuse violence and are the heart of God's logic. Jesus positions himself completely outside the cycle of violence and the thief sees it clearly: Jesus doesn't react to anyone, attacks no one, uses no verbal violence, accuses no one . . . His silence is not that of a beaten, bewildered, or powerless man; on the contrary, it is charged with another power, that of prayer, forgiveness, and love . . . In silence, Jesus does not cease to love; it is an active silence, strong with astonishing power, of which the thief takes full note. Christ's silence is stronger than all the waves of violence which devolve upon him.

Love and forgiveness make a way out of the cycle of violence; they make a way of escape from Satan's grip and are the sign of true liberty. The forgiveness Jesus asks of his Father will not be overcome by death; the Father's forgiveness subsists beyond death. This Jesus who forgives is far along the road to death, for sure, but he is dying free. To die attacking others is to die a slave to others' violence. To die forgiving is to die free, at peace . . . The thief is watching someone die free. This man right here, Jesus, is opening a door, and with him a new piece of evidence appears, that one may die without hatred, without cursing, without blaspheming; one may die loving God and others, die free, close to God, in God . . .

The thief in his silence is uniting with Christ in his; he is ready to follow Christ in his manner of dying, in his death, on this pathway of love which pardons, this pathway Christ sovereignly opens. This is a conversion; the thief converts.

Another kingdom

In the undercurrent of comments he hears continuing on and on against Jesus, the thief hears words like "Christ," "king," "Elijah," "the Christ of God." For sure it is all spoken in mockery, but what if it were true? What if the words written up in different languages above the cross were true, "This is the King of the Jews"?

This king is free from the grip of violence, free from the mockery, the blasphemies, the insults, and every other manifestation of hate; the King's prayer is full of love and knows forgiveness. What if, alongside human justice, there is another justice, that of this king? What if there is a kingdom for this king other than the kingdoms of the earth? A king must after all have a kingdom, and to judge by the King himself this kingdom must be one of love alone.

From high on his cross, the thief sees two worlds alongside each other, one in Christ who prays and forgives, the other which insults and curses.

The thief turns towards the King he is discovering; "Jesus, remember me when you come into your kingdom."

On one cross is a man at the tipping point of faith in the final hours of his life; this is the work of the Holy Spirit in him. While the other malefactor runs with the pack in the kingdom of the mob, the good thief opens his heart in silence to the King, that he may make his heart a portion of his kingdom. While Satan locks one malefactor into cursing, the Holy Spirit liberates the other into the kingdom of Christ.

Unceasing prayer

The thief is now able to understand Jesus' attitude to the assaults of violence, why he continues in silence, and what he is doing in this profound silence.

In the face of the violence, Jesus does not react in kind at all. There is no blow for blow, or insult for insult. He is silent and his silence is unbroken; his only words have been a prayer. What then must he be doing now in his silence, after this unleashing of aggression? What would he be doing other than continuing in prayer? All is clear to the good thief.

If Jesus' first words on the cross were prayer, it is because he is constantly in prayer. The first person he spoke to was his Father because he is always in communion with him through prayer. His request for forgiveness is not limited to events here at the cross; the prayer is not finished, but rather prolonged. This leaves no doubt; Jesus is continuing to ask of his Father forgiveness for the parting of his garments, the offering of vinegar, the sarcasms of the rulers, the soldiers' mockery, the blasphemy of the malefactor . . . In his silence, Christ intercedes unceasingly, "Father, forgive them, they know not what they do, they don't know what they are saying."

On the cross the thief pursues his silent meditation: if Jesus is praying for all these people, for this blasphemous rabble, might he not also be praying for me, his companion in pain, for me too, dying as I am like him . . . The thief's silence deepens, a silence full of love and thankfulness . . . In silence, the thief lets Jesus pray for him. Nobody had ever prayed for him; he marvels that this man should be praying as he is. What a wonder that this Son be nothing so much as prayer before his Father and that he should be interceding for me! Tears of joy don't disturb the silence as they fall.

A moment ago the thief had felt excluded from Christ's prayer; he suddenly perceives this is not so at all. Christ is interceding for him. The Spirit alone bears witness with our spirit that we are being carried before the Father in the Son's intercession (Rom 8:34). In his silence the thief gives himself over to the work of the three times Holy. God is so close: the Son is right there beside him on the cross; the Father is there, listening in the silence; the Spirit whispers to him in the depths of his heart.

Will the thief be forgiven by the Father without having asked, just because the Son has prayed for it? Is he to be blessed by the Father at the Son's request? The Spirit whispers in the depths of his heart and stirs within him, in the silence, a word he had never yet pronounced, "Abba."

What if Jesus' Father was also his Father? What if Jesus were more than a companion in torture—a brother? The Holy Spirit pursues his work in the thief's heart.

Jesus prays in silence for the thief; this is how he accompanies the dying. Don't forget, reader friend, that silent prayer finds a place alongside the dying. It is prayer that depends on the intercession of Christ, who intercedes for him without ceasing.

While there, on the cross, the thief is altogether silent; why has he not prayed in the silence? Why has he not, like Jesus, turned towards the Father and asked forgiveness for all his misdeeds? Has he perhaps never prayed in his life? When it comes to turning to the Father, he could not but discover the degree to which he is a sinner. The closer God comes, the greater the sinner he seems, and the more overwhelmed he feels by his faults, both known and unknown. If God pardons unknown faults at Christ's request, will he also pardon known faults? Don't all those deliberate faults render you unworthy to turn to God? The thief discovers himself to be unworthy of God's proximity, unworthy to pray. The fact is that the thief does not pray to the Father . . . Luke directs us to a different quarter.

At the thief's side is Jesus, who is praying. If so many unworthy people feel free to speak to Jesus, could not he, the unworthy thief, also speak to him? There he is, a few yards away, within easy range of the voice; even speaking softly he would hear. He may not have responded to anyone, but he must surely hear what is said.

Though the thief feels unworthy to pray to the Father, he will dare to pray to the Son; he suddenly feels free to pray . . .

Reader friend, of what are we witnesses in this portion of the Gospel, of the thief's death or his entrance into new life? Of his agony or his birth? What a wonderful Gospel, causing us to ponder the birth into life of a man at the hour of his death!

We could even say that we are witnesses of the resurrection of the thief. We remember that early in his Gospel, Luke reported the prophecy of the elderly Simeon spoken to Joseph and Mary, speaking of Jesus; "this child is for the fall and rising again of many in Israel" (2:34). This prophecy is being fulfilled on the cross; the fall is that of the blasphemer, the rising again is that of the good thief. The word used by Simeon to say "rising again" is *anastasis*, which also means "resurrection."

But before we listen to the thief's prayer, let us listen first to what he says to the other malefactor and see in the good thief a true disciple, a witness who stands in Jesus' defense.

The thief's witness

Since his trial, no one has defended Jesus; no disciple or anyone else has stood up to plead in his favor. Only false witnesses have stepped forward to spread their lies, and Jesus has not even defended himself. Even now, on the cross, he continues not to defend himself, not responding at all. Then the thief speaks up, after hearing the blasphemy from the other cross. He is the first to witness in Jesus' favor. The trial may be over, but that matters little; it is never too late to tell the truth; "this man has done nothing wrong!"

How did the thief know this about Christ? Was he one of his disciples? In any case he speaks as the disciples should have spoken, but as none of them had dared, afraid as they were of death. He, the thief, has no fear; he is free; he bears witness!

Satan caused Peter to fall, leading him to denial. He caused the malefactor to blaspheme, but is unable to cause the good thief to fail. If some servant girl had addressed to him the questions Peter replied "no" to, he would have replied "yes," yes, I know this man, he has done nothing wrong.

This first true testimony is a balm to Jesus' heart; finally somebody tells the truth.

How is it that this thief can speak the truth about Jesus when just yesterday he had never met him? How did he know Jesus had done nothing wrong? He knows it by an internal conviction which the Holy Spirit alone can give. The thief confesses his newborn faith; "I believe that he has done nothing wrong."

The thief's sermon

Not only does the thief bear witness but, more, he preaches, he evangelizes. He "rebukes" the blasphemer, Luke tells us. The thief reproaches the malefactor to make him aware of his mistake about Jesus, of his blasphemy, and to invite him to fear God. Right there, in just a few words, is a real sermon to produce repentance in the fear of God. Malefactors fear nobody, it is well known! They scorn fear, for sure, but, before God, wouldn't it be better that fear be acknowledged?

Men's justice has condemned us to torture on a cross, and this is just, our misdeeds surely merit it, says the thief. But what will the result of God's justice be when it comes to his verdict? At this moment Jesus is interceding and asking forgiveness for us. Be quiet! The Father may be about to answer his prayer and give his opinion. Be silent! The hour of our death approaches; we will soon appear before God! Do you not fear God?

We don't know the other malefactor's response to this preaching; Luke leaves him in silence. In this silence he will hear the good thief turn towards Christ to address him in prayer. He will also hear Christ's reply; he will be present at Christ's death . . . His silence is his secret with God, and it is not our place to penetrate the secret; we know one thing alone, that the Son intercedes for him before the Father, "Father, forgive him, for he knows not what he does."

The thief's prayer

"Jesus, remember me when you come into your kingdom"; perhaps this is the very first time that the good thief has attempted to pray? It is also the final, unique, and superb prayer which so many men and women have adopted in their turn. This prayer of such simplicity is the last thing the thief says; he dies praying, borne up by the promise Jesus has made in reply. A unique, superb prayer, which immediately receives its fulfillment in Jesus' response.

It is with all the weight of a criminal's existence that the thief speaks to Jesus. He puts forward nothing from his life, no good work, nothing of any merit; he doesn't even look for anything in the years gone by that might have pleased God. He brings himself to Christ as he is that day on the cross, in his dying hour; he abandons himself to grace alone: "Jesus, remember me when you come into our kingdom."

The vocative, "Jesus"

The first word the thief pronounces in this prayer is the name of Jesus.[1] Throughout the rest of Luke's Gospel, those who speak to Christ using a direct form of address always do so adding a title as a sign of respect.[2] The thief feels that Christ is so close to him that he addresses him with the greatest simplicity, "Jesus." This is the simplicity of those who share the same lot, the same pain, the same torture . . . But the thief is nevertheless not lacking in respect; he knows very well that in speaking of his "kingdom" he is speaking to a king. The absence of any title underlines the grandeur of this name; no title is great enough to be added to the name that, to him, says everything: "Jesus."

Does the thief perhaps remember that the name Jesus means "God saves"? Though he may not be aware of this, his request is replete with the reality; it is nothing less than salvation that he is asking of Jesus. The rulers, the soldiers mocked the name of Jesus saying, "Save yourself"; the thief is alone in speaking truthfully the reason for Jesus being called by that name. If he had said this word alone, his prayer would have retained all its poignancy; "Jesus."

Throughout the Passion, no one speaks to Jesus and calls him by name; no one honors him in the use of his own name; the thief is the first to do so, and will be the last. Again this is a salve, an ointment to Jesus' wounds; someone at his side calls him by his name; "Jesus."

Heaven and earth were awaiting this prayer to then bow down. The entire cosmos was waiting to bow its knee, waiting until someone pronounce the name that is above every name, as the apostle says (Phil 2:9).

---

1. "He said, 'Jesus, remember me.'" This is the generally adopted translation today. Some ancient translations prefer, "He said to Jesus, 'remember me,'" but often adding a new vocative, "He said to Jesus, 'Lord, remember me.'" These older translations depend on a manuscript tradition that goes back to Jerome, but lack the support of the most ancient manuscripts.

2. A possessed man says, "Jesus of Nazareth" (4:34); another says, "Jesus, Son of the Most High God" (8:28); the lepers say, "Jesus, Master"(17:13); and a blind man, "Jesus, Son of David" (18:38).

When the thief pronounces on the cross the name of Jesus, heaven bows, hell ceases its blasphemy and trembles, the earth cuts short its mockery and is silent. The cosmos is suddenly silent. There is no one beside the thief, who says, kneeling at least in his heart, "Jesus, remember me when you come into your kingdom."

In his prayer, the thief has not said, "Abba"; he has only said, "Jesus," but in this one word the grieved heart of the Father finds its consolation. Blessed thief, who the Spirit has enabled to find the word which rises up to the Father as a perfume of infinite sweetness.

"Remember me when you come into your kingdom"

There is no more astonishing prayer than that of the thief. He is a dying man, but he asks nothing relative to his present agony, nothing to help him across the redoubtable threshold of death; this is not his concern. He knows he will die beside the King, with him; this is enough. He could hope for no more beautiful death than that shared with the King.

In his prayer the thief sees himself already beyond death, when the King enters his kingdom. In his prayer the thief has projected himself beyond death.

Perhaps later, when the King is occupied with the affairs of his kingdom, he will forget this poor thief, his companion in misfortune. The thief is well aware that in a time of triumph one quickly forgets the moments of disgrace; this is why he now thinks it important to speak out his prayer.

"Remember me"; the thief asks nothing more, without specifying how he would like his remembrance realized. Remember me by having me sit at your right hand or your left, this had been the daring request of some! The thief has no hope of what some of the disciples had been able to dream; he is nothing more than a common criminal and not a familiar. It is already a great deal for such a malefactor to ask what he has; he dares ask nothing more; "Jesus remember me . . ." The thief leaves to the King the exercise of his grace in whatever manner he should choose.

Remember that I have spoken your name without any mockery! Remember that I silenced a blasphemer! No, the thief brings forward nothing of what he might have been able to do in Jesus' favor; he leaves everything to the King's grace. John the Baptist was unworthy to undo the straps of Christ's sandals; the thief knows for sure that he is unworthy to be crucified next to the King. He knows he is unworthy to speak to the King, but the love he has discovered in the crucified Jesus invites him to dare. The love which fills Christ releases the thief's prayer, makes him worthy and allows him to hope; Jesus, you who pray for your enemies, I am unworthy to be anything other than your enemy, but in your goodness, don't forget me.

The thief's faith

"When you come": to speak about the future at the hour of one's death is a feat of magnificent faith; such faith animates the thief. His sight sees beyond death; he doesn't deny death, he goes beyond it because he dies with Jesus.

For the thief, the future beyond death is summed up in one thing, the coming of Jesus. The beyond is centered solely on Jesus and his last coming. In this prayer the thief does not confess the first coming of Christ to earth but his last coming, his entering into his kingdom. The verb "to come" is the verb linked par excellence with the messianic hope. The prophets had announced this coming. John the Baptist had been the last to announce it; the thief's faith is the faith of all Israel and the faith of the church, the two to be united in the second coming.

"Save yourself and us too," the malefactor had said mockingly. The good thief, speaking in sincerity, asks nothing like that. He does not expect to be spared death and come down from the cross. He prepares to die and in his prayer places himself in the hands of the one to whom belongs the mystery of the beyond. He accepts his death because it is a just one in the eyes of man, and then he hands himself over to Jesus' judgment.

It is to the King that the thief speaks, which is to say, a person who exercises justice. You who are King, you will be my judge when you come into your kingdom. You are King, as I am a common criminal. Men have condemned me to death and I accept it; but those who condemned me have written on your cross that you are King and I believe it, and I wish to appear before your tribunal when you come into your kingdom. I remit my judgment into your hands; I will accept your verdict, whatever it might be, such is my confidence in you, you who I have seen ask your Father to forgive all your torturers. I commit myself to your grace . . .

Reader friend, if you should have occasion to sit with a dying person, be so bold as to pray with him about what lies beyond death, even if the dying person seems of little more value than a thief! Have the boldness to believe that Christ is present and that he receives the prayer of those who turn to him, who die with him, in him.

The thief on the cross teaches us to pray; there is no need for long or complex prayer to turn to Christ, no need for inflated titles or superlatives. A simple prayer is enough, with everyday words and unwavering faith.

The thief on the cross teaches us to die praying, with the heart turned towards the silent Christ. It is because Christ is silent that the thief speaks to him. His silence is always that of listening whenever some person, thief or not, speaks to him, pronouncing his name with confidence, "Jesus."

Christ's thirst quenched

In these moments of Jesus' agony, in the midst of the insults, someone approaches him offering him vinegar to drink, a new mockery which accentuates the suffering of crucifixion (see Ps 69:22; "when I was thirsty they gave me vinegar").

Luke doesn't mention Jesus' thirst on the cross, because he believes that he found in the thief matter to quench it; this prayer spoken with love and confidence is better than any glass of water. It flows from the thief's heart, a source from which Jesus can drink. This is something given him by the Father; he is not abandoned.

Christ's response

From his first moment on the cross Jesus has not responded to anyone, but this time he does. What a miracle for the thief who has dared address the King—the King replies! Indeed, Jesus' reply is the reply of a king, spoken with kingly authority. "In very truth, I tell you"; introduced in this way, what he says sounds like a decree. In the mouth of the King, this is a solemn royal pledge.

Jesus does not delay in answering; his reply is immediate, before death can accomplish its work, so that the thief may be carried through death by it. Jesus' response does not deny death but supersedes it.

Jesus could surely not forget the one who gave him to drink when he was thirsty. It is on the basis of the love shown in small actions and ordinary words that his judgment will proceed when he sits on his throne (see Matt 25:31–46). I was thirsty for love, thirsty for the trust of one close to me; you knew how, through your prayer, to quench my thirst—"Today you will be with me in paradise."

To a heart which is open to him, Jesus opens the door to paradise. It is easier to open the door to paradise that to open the door to the heart of those who blaspheme. You, who open your heart to me, to you I open a door that no man can close (Rev 3:8).

At his baptism, heaven opened before the humility of Christ in prayer; here paradise opens before the humble prayer of the thief. It is not that death is bypassed but that it is a place in which Jesus opens a door onto paradise.

"Today"

This word is to be taken at face value. It is the "today" of the thief's death, the "today" he is living in all its reality, but it is also an eternal today, the today of God, which has neither evening nor morning. In Jesus' reply, the today of men and the today of God are united. As mysterious as this may be, Jesus will, on the same day, both descend into hell and enter paradise. He will descend into hell with the one who has blasphemed, and enter paradise with the one who has prayed with faith; he will thus accompany each one in death, as he alone knows how; he dies with each of them.

In his reply, Jesus brings into the present what in the thief's mouth is future. It is indeed today, he says, that I am entering into my kingdom. I am in fact King, a crucified, ridiculed, and blasphemed king, but a king all the same and it is with my royal authority that I say to you, "Today you will be with me in paradise. As truly as you are here with me on a cross, today you will be with me in paradise."

Then there was darkness over the whole land

With the darkness, it is Satan who draws near. The power of Satan (Acts 26:18) is the power of darkness. Jesus knew this time would be daunting indeed, and had stated the previous day to those who came to arrest him, "This is your hour and of the power of darkness" (Luke 22:53).

It is an intimidating darkness that might overturn the new faith of the thief; an intimidating darkness that would last three whole hours. The sun hides its face. The sudden fall of night in the middle of the day enforces silence. The mockers are silent; their insults cease. In the silence there is the calming of the din; but for the thief an intimidating aspect of the darkness is that he can no longer see Jesus. The silence is also that of God; there only remains faith in all its fragility, assailed by the power of darkness. To believe without seeing; to believe without understanding; to only believe . . .

At the same time as the darkness, death approaches. He will have to die during the night, die in the silence that covers the land, in the silence of God.

Death approaches, but Jesus and the thief are still side by side. Together they will die in silence. Jesus is sustained by the thief's prayer which still resonates in his heart; the thief is sustained by Jesus' response which still resonates in his heart. The two together are enveloped in the darkness. What is God doing in the silent darkness?

The silence is so great that it is possible to hear an unexpected, surprising sound! The thief nevertheless understands it well; the veil of the temple has been ripped in two . . . and there is no doubt that this ripping is a sign of mourning; someone is expressing through this action his pain at the death of a loved one; there is no rending of a garment otherwise! Who is it then, alone, in mourning amidst the darkness?

Then Jesus raises his voice to be sure that the thief hears; he lifts his voice to make clear the presence and identity of the mourner; "Father!"

Jesus' final prayer

"Father, into your hands I commit my Spirit." What the thief hears from Jesus' mouth approximates to a psalm, though the thief perhaps does not know this. The psalmist also said to God, "into your hands I commit my spirit" (Ps 31:5), but without naming as "Father" the one he addresses, calling him only "Lord" (31:2, 6, 10, 15, 18). The prayer is different with Jesus, of a different depth. The thief hears the Son pray to the Father.

"Father, into your hands I commit my Spirit." This prayer of Christ, his last, is a moment of great trinitarian intensity, of love beyond any other; the Son commits the Spirit to the Father . . .

At the baptism the Father committed the Spirit to the Son with an expression of great and deep intimate love; "You are my beloved Son; in you I repose all my affection." Now the Son commits the Spirit to the Father as he breathes his last in an equally deep prayer of love.

When Jesus prayed at his baptism, heaven opened; now, when he prays on the cross, paradise opens. Satan, defeated, was unable to disturb the communion of trinitarian love; the thief escapes him and will follow Christ.

With his last prayer, Christ teaches the thief how to die and through this teaching accompanies him in death. We may die freely committing our spirit to God. For the thief, this is a discovery, the uncovering of a pathway of liberty. Death has no power. The thief may freely offer his spirit to God in a supreme liberty which despoils death of its prize.

The death of Christ

Of the three crucified men, Jesus is the first to die, as John tells us (19:32–33). The thief is therefore present, still alive to silently accompany the King in his death, an inexpressible moment for the thief, an intense moment.

Then "all those who were there in the crowd for this deed, seeing what came to pass, turned away, beating their breast." Golgotha emptied. For the thief the silence increases! Nevertheless, he rests on the word to which he clings; the promise Jesus made him can only bring assurance.

The thief does not feel forsaken; he knows that the King has left first, gone to prepare a place for him in his kingdom (see John 14:2).

He does not feel abandoned by God; he knows the Father is there, his garment rent, to hear his prayer, ready to receive his spirit when the moment comes to commit it to him.

He does not feel abandoned by the Holy Spirit; immediately after Jesus' death, the thief hears a man at the foot of the cross say these simple words, "Certainly this was a just man" (v. 47). How these words agree with the thoughts of the thief! This confession of the centurion is balm to the thief's heart. The Holy Spirit alone could have brought the soldier to say this.

The thief's death

All those who were at Golgotha go their way, each beating his breast . . . No one will be present at the death of the thief. The handful of women who stood at a distance kept their silence and finally left. Someone returns before nightfall; they determine that the thief was not yet dead and break his legs, and spirit and body are parted . . .

No one was there for the thief's death! He dies in the secret place of God . . .

No one knows if he prayed.

No one can tell if he committed his spirit into the hands of the Father.

No one knows if he cried "Abba" or "Jesus" with his final breath.

No one knows except God . . .

All that remains for us are the wonderful words left him by the Son as provision[3] to conduct him to the Father; "Today you will be with me in paradise."

---

3. The word used in the French denotes *viaticum*, a reference to an element of Roman Catholic practice in the giving of Holy Communion to the dying. The meaning is a provision for a journey. (Trans.)

CHAPTER 2

The Psalm of Descent into Hell

Many centuries before Christ, perhaps a thousand years, a man was dying, one Heman, who fulfilled the function of singer in the temple in Jerusalem (1 Chr 6:33). All his life he had stood before God in the sanctuary and had grown in his faith and love for God to such a degree that we can speak of a real intimacy.

Whether it is a sign of great humility I really don't know, but what is sure is that we have nothing other from Heman than this one psalm, no other prayer than this, pronounced as he died. It is preserved for and transmitted to us in what is now Psalm 88. This familiar of the temple, steeped in the psalms by virtue of his office, fashioned by prayer, left nothing of himself besides his dying prayer. This is a cry, difficult to bear, it is true, because of the great suffering it contains, but also a cry of love and of faith which never ceases to amaze me in the very beautiful intimacy with God it lays bare.

I intend to simply work through the text step by step, verse by verse, to the silence of its ending in which there remain mingled, as they have been from the outset, unbearable suffering and the purity of faultless faith.

There are numerous psalms of supplication, but this one is quite astonishing since it is one of the few that does not break into praise. Generally speaking, in the Psalter, the prayers of supplication pass, at one moment or another, from complaint into thanksgiving, without one always being able to know what God has done to suddenly enable the psalmist to express joy and thankfulness (cf. 7:18; 13:6; 22:23; etc.). There is nothing of this in Heman's prayer, which pleads with God until its final word, until the last breath, without obtaining the least response or sign that would lead to thanksgiving. It is in this that the psalm is difficult to understand.

Besides this, and this is what makes it so remarkable, the psalm is the expression of an extraordinary faith. Heman dies without weakening in his prayer, without doubting God's presence at his side and without ever pulling away from him. At no moment does he interrupt his prayer to address those around him. At no point does he call on anyone other than God, not even his own soul, as happens with other psalmists.[1] Heman dies in prayer. The silence that prolongs his final word is a silence full of prayer.

Here is the psalm.

> *A song, a psalm for the sons of Korah, to the lead singer from Heman the musician: to the accompaniment of the flute.*[2]

1. Lord, God of my salvation,

    I cry through the day, but it is night in your presence.

2. *Let my prayer come unto you;*

    Open your ear to my supplication,

3. *Because my soul is full of troubles*

    And my life is joined to the place of the dead.

4. *I am counted among those who go down to the pit;*

    I am like a man with no more to sustain him.

5. *I am free among the dead,*

    With the deceased who are laid in the tomb,

---

1. See Ps 6:8 for an address to enemies, 22:23 to friends, and 104:1 where David speaks to his own soul.

2. In the French this introduction is considered the first verse of the psalm but the translation here follows the traditional English numbering and is a direct translation of the author's French. (Trans.)

The Psalm of Descent into Hell

With those of whom you have no memory,
Those who are cut off from your hand.

6. *You have laid me in the depths of the pit,*
   In the darkness, in the abyss.

7. *Your fury weighs down on me.*
   All your waves overwhelm me . . .

   Pause

8. *You have removed my intimates far from me!*
   You have made me repugnant to them!
   I am imprisoned and there is no way out.

9. *My eyes grow weak because of my suffering.*
   All the day, Lord, I call upon you,
   As I open my hands towards you.

10. *Will you do a miracle for the dead?*
    Shall corpses rise up to praise you?

    Pause

11. *Will your faithfulness be proclaimed in the tomb?*
    And your truth in the kingdom of death?

12. *Will your miracles be known in the darkness?*
    And your justice in the land where all is forgotten?

13. *As for me, Lord, I implore your help.*
    In the morning my prayer will come before you.

14. *Why, Lord do you push away my soul?*
    Why do you hide your face from me?

15. *I am overwhelmed, condemned from my childhood.*
    I have undergone your terrors, I am at my very end.

16. *Your anger goes over me.*

> *Your terrors reduce me to silence.*
> 17. *They swirl around me like water, all the day,*
>   *And they close over me, all together.*
> 18. *You have removed from me friend and familiar.*
>   *My only companion is darkness.*

LORD, I cry

The first word of the psalm is the name of God![3] It is a miracle to be able to join one's cry to the name of God. So many cries are unheard, or they remain blocked up or smothered . . . Heman tethers his cry to God's name and secures it there. The entire psalm clings to the name with the strength of this cry.

All the psalms whose first word is the name of God are psalms full of a great love for God. Heman here sets himself to cry out with all the intensity of his love.

At the same time there is something in this cry that brushes with blasphemy because Heman is at death's door; he has, no doubt, one foot in the grave, and perhaps both! Biblically, it was inconceivable that one would pronounce the name of the God of the living when within the kingdom of the dead; the name was not be pronounced by impure lips, and still less so by the lips of the dying; death makes anything that touches it unclean.

What then is the truth about this psalm—should it be seen as blasphemy or miracle? If it were blasphemy it certainly would not have been retained in the Psalter, so it is therefore a miracle! The miracle is the great faith of Heman, which goes so far as to run the risk of blasphemy, out of love for the one he has loved all his life. He must

---

3. The divine name is represented by the Hebrew consonants YHWH, which are conventionally rendered in English by the title LORD, placed in capital letters. (Trans.)

feel himself particularly close to God to dare pronounce his name on his deathbed. Heman is so familiar with God, so intimate even, that he dares say what so many other dying people would hesitate to say. Though at the heart of death, he knows himself to be close to the heart of God, so close that he has no fear of blaspheming. In complete confidence, he looses his cry.

God of my salvation

This expression is a magnificent confession of faith; it shows that Heman has personally appropriated what was given to his people as a whole; the savior of Israel is also Heman's savior. There is no other savior than this, whatever the danger might be.

In what way was God's salvation to be manifest? Would it be God saving Heman by healing him and snatching him back from death? It could be, since nothing is impossible with God. Would God save Heman through death, beyond death, without healing him? This also is possible with God. Whatever the case, Heman knows that death will not have the last word since it belongs to God; he can overrule death and cause one to taste, after death, an eternity of life. Whatever form of salvation God may grant, Heman has confidence and commits himself to his Lord, the God of his salvation.

It is quite frequent that a dying person calls out for a loved one who has previously crossed the boundary of death; a father, a mother, or some other person who may be waiting on the other side of life. At death's door this is one way of seeking aid. Heman doesn't call on his father or mother . . . the only one to whom he turns and the only one who can help is God himself; Lord, he cries, you are the God of my salvation and to you alone I address my prayer; I commit my life into your hands.

I cry through the day, but it is night in your presence

Heman cries out at the heart of the day, in full daylight; it is no impediment that for him the day has become dark. He knows he is in God's presence, but this presence seems to him as dark as the night. God is light, for sure, but he makes himself so unseen that this light is become for Heman a thick darkness; and this darkness will not leave him, not for a moment. It has accompanied him for so long that he reaches the point of saying, before giving place finally to silence, that it has become his intimate, "My intimate companion, the darkness!"

"It is night in your presence." In this avowal there is a profound pain, which is added to that of approaching death.

The Hebrew word chosen by Heman to express the presence of God is one that implies a great proximity, similar to that between the man and the woman at beginning of creation; it is the word used in Gen 2:18 to say that for the man the woman is his intimate, his very self.

If Heman proposes to cry out before God, it is not because God is distant; it is not to overcome any distance but because the pain of the night is too intense. When a baby cries in the arms of its mother it is not to call for someone who could not be any closer but rather to express the intensity of its suffering. Heman is not unaware of the attentive and loving presence of God, but he does not prevent the pain he feels from issuing in the cries he cannot hold back.

It is night, but in the middle of the day. Will this night make way for a new day, a new dawn? Heman firmly believes so and manages to say in a simple magnificence of hope, "In the morning my prayer will come before you." Assuredly, the night will be unable to prevent the dawn from spreading its light. Heman's pain is big with a secret hope.

The Psalm of Descent into Hell

My prayer will come unto you

"My prayer"; it is marvelous to hear this word because it is this which gives Heman's cry its greatest beauty. Whatever is said in the cry, it is not going out into the void, to be lost in nothingness; the cry is a prayer, which means that God is there to hear it. For Heman there is no doubt of this; as a musician in Jerusalem, a man of prayer, an intimate of God's, he is indwelt by the certainty that God hears his prayer. The Jerusalem musician is confronted by God's silence, but has the conviction that the silence is that of someone who is listening closely.

Will Heman have the strength to cry out for long? Probably not, but this matters little. Even if it turns into groaning or simple silence, Heman has no doubt, his prayer will reach God. It may be night, but the man of prayer knows that God is there in the darkness, and that it is not necessary to wait until the morning to be heard. It is enough that God inclines his ear, and this is what Heman asks.

Incline your ear to my supplication

Heman chooses his words perfectly. "Incline your ear" is not something one says to a stranger. The phrase is only used in Hebrew within a close relationship (as servant and master) or intimacy (son and father) (cf. Prov 4:10; Ps 45:11). The ear requested would never be indifferent, not inattentive, but that of a loving, caring listener.

"Incline your ear"; the expression is very just—when close, one ear is enough, but when far away, by contrast, you need to incline both! This manner of speaking shows us that for Heman God is near. God is not deaf. What Heman asks of him is close attention, and, no doubt, great affection.

"Incline your ear" is the only imperative in this psalm, the only request Heman addresses to God. He seeks nothing from God other than an increasing closeness and attentiveness, to be heard perfectly.

He is aware that his prayer will little by little lose its intensity as death approaches. May God make himself more immediate than death!

The word translated as "supplication" requires some explanation because it cannot be satisfactorily rendered in English.[4] The Hebrew word (*rinnah*) means both "supplication" and "exultation," which is an extraordinary paradox. The same word means both complaint and joy; this is the paradox we have to accept. Even if untranslatable, there is no need for us to choose between the two meanings, but instead we must try to understand how Heman's complaint can be mingled with joy, and what this joy is that is expressed within the grief.

The dictionaries in fact specify that the primary meaning is that of exultation. The verb from which our word derives means firstly "to shout for joy." In Heman's remarks there is something of the fabulous; his cry is one of pain, but not that alone; even if the pain is great it cannot efface the joy. Perhaps this is why Heman asks God to incline his ear, because he will be able to hear the joy behind the suffering; no ear other than God's would be attuned enough to understand this prayer. Heman knows this and so speaks to no one other than God. What then of our ability to hear? We have no trouble understanding Heman's pain, but when it comes to the joy, this is another matter! May God help us to incline our ear, our better ear, to understand this man's jubilation.

What is Heman's joy, this tenuous joy, so darkened by his complaint, which requires the closest attention to be heard? I believe it is the joy of knowing God to be present, even if unseen in the night. It is the joy of being yet able to pray, even though the darkness is pressing and heavy.

The suffering is too great to allow the joy to be expressed, but if God will incline his ear, he will perceive what cannot be expressed. He will understand in the supplication, the groaning, in the death rattle or in the dying man's final breath—he will understand the silent joy . . . Indeed, God's ear will hear.

---

4. As in French. (Trans.)

The Psalm of Descent into Hell

This secret joy, which cannot speak itself but is implicit in the supplication from the first to the last word, explains the peculiarity of the psalm, that it never shifts from complaint to praise. Such a change has no place because Heman does not move between the two; he experiences both, constantly. This is both the beauty and the difficulty of the psalm; for us, we must at no point forget that in the ever-present supplication there is an inexpressible joy, just as present.

As a preparation for this, the title of the psalm requires that it be played "on the flute"; in Israel the flute was played at weddings as well as funerals. Heman chose his instrument well; his death involves an inexpressible nuptial joy.

My soul is assailed by troubles

Heman's suffering is not only physical; in fact, there is no word which actually expresses any physical pain. The pain is internal, in the depths of his being, as he goes down into death. Heman's soul can no longer take the piling of trouble upon trouble; he is full, saturated.

What are these troubles, these ills? The Hebrew term designates both the evil of which Heman is himself the author, his sin, and the evil he must undergo. Heman doesn't specify whether he has had enough of being a victim or if it his guilt which troubles him. The image of being assailed does seem to suggest that he is thinking of the evil he is forced to swallow, evil coming from the outside and of which he is a victim; but while he never confesses any fault to God, neither does he present himself as innocent. He seems to situate himself outside the issue of guilt; he has simply had enough of trouble, whatever its nature or source. He is suffering and that is all; this is enough to turn to God, the God of his salvation, and ask him to intervene: Lord, I am a sinner for sure, but whether innocent or guilty, don't stop there. I am suffering. My pain is so great that it has taken over my whole being, to the depths of my soul. I am suffering embodied. I don't know where it comes from but I am full of it to the point of sickness. I can do no more. Draw near to me in your goodness and have pity on me, O God of my salvation.

My life is joined to the place of the dead

Again there is a paradoxical expression which speaks of both life and death, that Heman is still alive and yet already dead. I believe we need to accept the paradox, as it speaks of a man at once living and already dead and descending into hell; the rest of the prayer is set within this paradox.

The dwelling place of the dead is denoted in Hebrew by a feminine word, Sheol. In biblical imagery, Sheol has a stomach and the dead go down into the place of the dead as into a stomach. Not into a womb from which life can emerge, but into a stomach to be digested and reduced to nothing.

The etymology of the word Sheol shows it to be place of interrogation (*Shā'al*), of being questioned, by God no doubt, about one's acts. Heman does not see it in this way; he does not see God as someone to whom he must give account; this is not what he expects and instead it is he who poses a great range of questions. This might be a form of insolence, an attitude which is at least blasphemous, subverting God's majesty, but this really is not something that springs from the psalm. Heman is a close friend of God, intimate enough to ask questions as a friend questions a friend.

But we should wait; for the moment, Heman has not yet begun his questions but limits himself to describing his experience, his descent into the place of the dead.

The Psalm of Descent into Hell

**I am counted among them
that go down into the pit** _____

This phrase begins with a passive structure that doesn't make it clear whether it is Heman who considers himself among the dead. Is it the point of view of those around him, either his friends or his enemies, the friends to deplore, the enemies rejoicing? Heman does not specify. The phrase is so fluid one could even ask if it is God who is thought to count him among the dead; but Heman does not allow himself to say this. His silence on this point is full of his respect and love for God.

"To go down into the pit"; Heman does not speak of the tomb but of the pit. He is not intending to be vulgar, but he does speak crudely without sparing his divine interlocutor and appealing to him in his love. He is sufficiently free with God to tell him his suffering in the crudest words; Heman reveals both his pain at being thought no more than a common corpse, and his intense longing for God's compassion.

**I am like a man with no
more to sustain him** _____

There are many words in Hebrew that can be used for a man. Heman here chooses one which does not suggest a man in his weakness but, on the contrary, a man in his strength. This seems to indicate that it is not an elderly man speaking but rather a man in the prime of his life. To his sufferings, therefore, we must add that of a premature death. He is not dying "full of days," as an old man would say, but "full of troubles," as he has just told God, taken before his time. Everything has brought him to the end of his strength, while he is still only in the midst of his days.

The word "sustain" or "sustenance" chosen by Heman (*'eyāl*) is one that derives from the word for God (*El*); this indicates that the help he hopes for is from God and not men. If Heman is expressing his lack it is only to God he can speak. Here is a man at the end of his own strength, who is also deprived of the strength of God. What remains for him but to go down into death?

I am free among the dead

This is an expression most modern translators handle poorly when the meaning is in fact clear. The oldest translation is that of the Septuagint; it thoroughly respects the Hebrew text, and we should do the same.

Heman affirms, then, that he is free among the dead. What exactly does this mean? Biblically, the place of the dead is the kingdom of silence (Ps 31:18), where no one speaks. Heman, however, discovers that he still enjoys the freedom to speak and even to pray. Is this some gift unknown to any other who is dead? Perhaps, though, Heman doesn't know; what is true is that he feels free before God. He uses this freedom in the best of ways and gives himself entirely to prayer, without excess, without revolt, without going beyond due measure in any way and without taking advantage of God's friendship. He is free as a friend is free in his speech with a friend.

His affirmation of freedom is also perhaps a way of inviting God to intervene in his favor. Heman seems, in effect, to wish to say that he is free of corruption, not yet affected by the decomposition of his dead body. We must remember that in Israel the corruption, the decomposition of a body was not considered to begin until the third day after death. This is what lies behind Lazarus' sister, Martha, saying to Jesus that it was the fourth day and that her brother's body already stank (John 11:39). For Heman the descent into the place of the dead had only just taken place and he is therefore still free of corruption. The door to life is still open; God could still step in. Heman lets him know this by speaking of his freedom.

Those whom you remember no more

Can God forget a loved one, a faithful believer, a friend? This is unthinkable and it would be close to blasphemous to assert such a thing! The Bible affirms constantly that God does not forget his own (1 Sam 1:11; Isa 49:15; Amos 8:7; Ps 9:12, etc.). It would be very dramatic to be forgotten by God!

This doesn't prevent certain writers at times asking themselves or asking God if he had forgotten them (Ps 13:1; 42:9; Lam 5:20). Nevertheless, such thoughts never go beyond the state of being questions to then become affirmations. Heman is alone in daring to cross the boundary into assertion; "those whom you remember no more."

Heman touches on blasphemy, but does not in fact blaspheme. Effectively what he says is spoken to someone of whose infinite love he is aware, and it is this love that he seeks to impress and turn towards him. Free in his speech with God, Heman is not toying with blasphemy; he wishes only to induce God to give him a sign of his limitless love.

You have laid me in the depths of the pit

Heman considers himself as already dead and buried, and is not exaggerating in this. He has been well and truly buried. At the same time he discovers something of which he would doubtless never have dreamed; if there had already been a burial, it had been conducted by God. This is unprecedented and passes understanding! God himself has laid him in the tomb! There was no one closer than God to fulfill this role! God himself had not recoiled at the defilement of contact with the corpse! Should Heman complain at having been buried, or marvel because God himself had buried him? Should he speak to God in supplication or in exultation? Both, for sure!

If God had abased himself to lay Heman in the tomb, even in a simple pit, should bitter tears be wept because of the pit, or tears of great sweetness because of the hands of the one who buried his friend? The word "lay" used by Heman is one that can denote great gentleness; it is the word used in Gen 46:4 to describe the hand that is laid on the eyes of the dying to close them; again in Gen 48:14, for the hand laid on a child in blessing; and finally in Ruth 4:16 to speak of the love of a woman who lays a child upon her breast.

If God has buried Heman with his own hands, it is because he is attached to him by a bond of love that passes understanding. To speak of God's infinite friendship with Heman is far from exaggerated. "You have laid me in the depths of the pit"; these words are spoken with a great sadness mingled with the great sweetness of a love without measure. Only tears can accompany such words, tears both sweet and bitter at once.

In an inexpressible way, Heman has felt the very hands of God take hold of him and lay him in the pit. It is an inexpressible closeness of God! Certainly Heman is in the depths of the pit, "in the darkness, in the abyss," but nothing can efface from his heart what he has felt, God's embrace! Assuredly, God could never forget one he had himself buried; not even a man could forget someone he has been at pains to lay in the pit . . .

"The pit," not "the tomb"! This word may surprise in a context of such intimacy, but the word "pit" is nevertheless not charged with any sense of vulgarity; it underlines Heman's extreme pain without in any way detracting from his love for God.

"You have laid me in the pit." Extreme pain is mixed with a wonderment just as great. Heman's only request addressed to his friend is still "incline your ear to me." You whose love has extended to laying me in the pit, don't turn away your ear, because this is the deepest of pits; keep your ear turned always towards me, when my prayer is reduced to silence; you will be able still to hear my pain in the silence, as well as my secret joy at being loved so well.

Before Heman, just one other person had known the privilege of being buried by God, Moses, God's friend. God had buried him alone, without any witness; so well was he hidden that to this day no one knows the place of Moses' grave (Deut 34:6). God could no more forget Heman than he could Moses.

Heman's remarks are so astonishing that the first translators felt bound to soften them a little. To touch a dead person is to become unclean! The Septuagint translators were therefore offended at the idea of God becoming unclean; they were also perhaps shocked at the notion that God could be likened to a gravedigger, so they subtly modified the text to avoid the risk of blasphemy; badly put out by Heman's boldness, they have translated it simply by "I have been laid in the depths of the pit . . ."

Before sinking into silence, Heman pronounces a few more words without being able to make it to the end of his sentence; "your fury weighs down on me; all your waves overwhelm me . . ."

"It is on me that your fury weighs down"

On me and on no one else . . . God's fury might well have fallen on Heman's enemies, thus saving his friend from death. But Heman knows of no adversary and certainly names none; no enmity appears anywhere in the psalm. Everything that passes is between Heman and God.

"Your fury"; by mentioning God's anger, Heman implicitly recognizes his sin. If he has no enemy, then God's anger could not be being expressed through enemies, and its direct expression could only have been provoked by Heman's own sin (Ps 6:1; 38:1–21).

Nevertheless, God's friend does not confess his sin, but neither does he seek to justify himself. He strives simply to bear up under the divine anger, but without success, weakened as he is and unworthy as he feels before the love of God.

Your fury "weighs me down, presses on me"; after the mention of burial, Heman's remark seems to describe the moment when the tombstone is laid down. God's anger is as weighty as a tombstone on a corpse!

All your waves have gone over me

The mention of waves evokes the presence of the chaos which endeavors to take over the earth (Gen 1:2). The original chaos is the adversary of God and the abyss of death into which Heman knows himself to be sinking.

Heman is so worn down he is unable to finish his sentence; he has no more strength to pronounce the complement of the verb. He reaches the end of his strength before he reaches the end of his sentence. He sinks into silence as into chaos.

But though chaos exists, it is no longer truly an adversary; God has mastered it. The waves are now those of God, who is master of the situation. Heman says *"your* waves," not "the waves"; in this phrase Heman's faith in the total power of God is apparent.

Heman doesn't manage to finish what he is saying; he is sinking, certainly, but he is sinking into the waves of the chaos God has mastered. Heman can let himself fall, abandoning himself into the hands of the one from whom nothing escapes.

"All" your waves; this is the extreme pain of someone who believes himself to be bearing the full weight of God's anger; his lengthy supplication is permeated with this.

Heman also becomes aware that no one other than God is involved in his death. This makes him dependent not on his enemies but on his friend. Throughout his life Heman has been able to affirm his confidence in the interventions of the God of his salvation. If God is now intervening by leading him into death, why not continue to keep faith? He may lack strength to pursue his prayer, but in the silence his prayer does not cease . . . The only one of whom Heman can complain is God; but the only one who can receive his complaint . . . is God. This is the great confidence of one who, despite everything, knows himself to be in the hands of his friend; his secret exultation is present throughout.

Pause

In the silence of this pause, Heman has no more strength to speak, but he retains the ability to listen. In the night that surrounds him he can see nothing, but it is still possible for him to hear. He knows that in this darkness there is no enemy and that he can always count on the presence of some friend or some loved ones who have perhaps come to accompany him in his last moments. Discreetly, his friends have been silent until now, leaving him to pray. If he keeps quiet now, no doubt he will hear one or another give some sign of their friendly presence . . .

During the pause, Heman scrutinizes the silence around him . . .

In the silence of this pause, he is unable to perceive anything of his loved ones' presence. He understands that he is absolutely alone, that there is no one at his side; what cruel absence!

This painful discovery draws from Heman the rest of his prayer. He gathers all his strength to tell God about the new suffering.

You have removed my intimates far from me

The absence of any enemy is a source of peace, but the absence of friends is a source of trouble and pain. Heman until now has not mentioned his friends because he believed them to be there. Perhaps they had been, early in his agony, perhaps they were still there when he began to pray; but when he interrupted his prayer to gather fresh strength from his friends, the silence reveals their absence.

What has happened? Have his friends left him to sink? Have they left him willingly?

Had they no stomach to bear with his agony? Heman is so sure of their friendship that he sees no betrayal in them. If they have left him, it must be that someone has made them. Only one person could have done that.

Heman now dares speak to the one who is responsible for this defection to tell him, quite freely, his doubled pain, that of realizing his friends' departure and that of the discovery that God could have thus made the ones he was counting on leave.

"You have removed my intimates far from me"; the pain of emptiness is caused by God himself.

In the silence of the pause, Heman has become aware of the absence; he has also understood that God has acted to take his friends away.

You have rendered me repugnant to them

This phrase could also be translated as "you have made me an abomination to them," noting that the word abomination is a plural word, as if to make it superlative; "you have made me absolutely repugnant to them!"

Heman understands; he is absolutely insupportable in the sight of his friends. This must make him feel terrible. His physical condition is such as to make his friends feel sick; the manner of his death is so unbearable that everyone has left. We don't know what Heman is dying of, but there is something in the sight of it which is nauseating.

Heman has nothing to reproach his friends for, and this is not what he does. He understands their absence; who can bear the unbearable? Their leaving is so painful that Heman has the strongest of reasons to complain, but also, and this is where his supplication doubles as secret exultation, he is aware that there does remain one person present! There is one who can bear the unbearable; God is always there!

He has not left Heman during his silent pause; his dying state has not sickened God. To him he is not repugnant; he is not an abomination. What relief to be able to count on God's being there; this unique presence becomes an inestimable comfort. What a gift, to be able still to turn to God when there is no one else. The intimate friend becomes still more so. If a wisp of rebellion has shown up, intimacy with God causes it to disappear.

Until this moment Heman has enjoyed great liberty of speech, but he has felt this, thinking that his friends heard his prayer. With friends around one can pray freely, though not entirely so; there is an avoidance of anything that might damage the friendship and great care in the choice of words, which might offend the friends' ears. Now that he knows his friends are not there, Heman has no reason for concern about their reactions to some of his thoughts. He is absolutely alone with God, so what he is now going to be able to say will not meet with any reaction from others, no approval or disapproval. The tone of his prayer can therefore take on even greater frankness, in profound sincerity and full liberty.

The discovery of his friends' absence explains the alterations we will see in Heman's prayer. For example, with them there, he would not have dared speak of the repugnance they feel towards him. The fact is that before his pause, when he believed them there, he had not mentioned the smell he might be producing or the state of physical disability he offers to the sight.

Now he knows he is alone, Heman will be able to tell God things he has never said before. Prayer will be made in entire freedom, from the deepest depths of his heart.

I am imprisoned and there is no way out

"I am free," Heman had said before his pause. "I am imprisoned," he says now! How can he say such contradictory things?

As long as he believed his friends were with him, Heman made an effort to sound confident so as not to disquiet them any more. Before friends it is fine at times to exaggerate one's hopes and not disturb them with one's despair; to inflate one's own confidence and deflate their disquiet. In respect for his friends, Heman had dissembled his suffering with reassurances; "I am free among the dead." But with God, alone with him, it is no longer necessary to carry on in this way. Friends can be fooled, but God certainly can't. The underlying truth cannot be hidden from him.

It's true that Heman is genuinely free when it comes to speech; he is free to think, free to pray, but this genuine liberty is found in the kingdom of the dead, where he is held captive. He is free but within the dwelling place of the dead from which he cannot come forth; "I am imprisoned and there is no way out."

It is from the depths of the pit that Heman's supplication rises. As harrowing as it might be, the complaint is nevertheless unable to destroy the secret jubilation within the psalm; the complaint remains a prayer, despite everything. Supplication and exultation remain inseparable; "Lord, I am imprisoned in the place of the dead but you are still listening to my prayer. You are there, with me, present in my prison. It is night in this dungeon, but you are there in my night. I can again turn to you without even needing to cry out . . . to you, the God of my salvation."

My eyes grow weak because of my suffering

In the deepest depths of the pit, in the place of the dead, in this prison with no way out, the darkness does not even allow you to distinguish between day and night; but this matters little! Even if God were to set a light blazing it would be of no service because Heman feels the onset of blindness. No doubt it is because of this fading sight that he didn't notice the absence of his friends. It was only the silence that revealed it.

In the deepest depths of the pit, the suffering is extreme. What is the source of the suffering? Heman has no need to specify. It is clear: God must surely remember Heman's final words before his silence, "all *your* waves, *you* overwhelm me . . ."

In this extremity of suffering, just one recourse remains to Heman, that of prayer. This is what he is doing, and will continue to do as long as he can.

All day long, **Lord,** I call out to you and open my hands towards you _____

Heman's strength is slowly draining away as he prays, but this matters little; he continues! He no longer cries out as at first, but simply calls; no longer stretching out his hands towards God but merely opening them.

The customary gesture for prayer in Israel was to open one's hands, lifting them towards heaven. Heman no longer has strength to lift his, so he contents himself with opening them. But it is of little importance; this is enough to express his attitude of prayer. When he can no longer speak and is silent, and even when he has breathed his last, his hands will remain open, and they will prolong his prayer as long as they remain so, which is to say, perhaps, eternally!

This is a marvel; death has the power to cause the hands of those who have raised them in prayer to fall back to their sides, but it cannot close the hands of the dying who have opened them; neither can it close the eyes of the dying which are turned towards heaven, or the mouth of those whose final breath has been committed to God . . . Thank you, Lord, for making death powerless before prayer . . .

Heman knows it; his eyes are certainly failing, but they stay turned towards God. He has opened his hands; they will remain open and will maintain his prayer even beyond death. Death will not have the last word over his prayer even though it imposes silence . . .

Before he becomes finally silent, Heman decides to ask God some questions. When he thought his friends were around he didn't ask any. Perhaps he dared not? Perhaps he feared his friends would try to answer in God's place, as friends often do; even the best intentioned friends endeavor to speak for God!

The friends are not there. If someone should have the last word, that right surely belongs to God. It is enough to ask him questions. When Heman no longer has the strength to speak, he will still be able to hear God's replies. Only one voice can bring joy now, that of the closest of intimates. The sound of God's voice; that is what he awaits . . .

Will you do a miracle among the dead?
Shall corpses rise up to praise you? _____

These two questions are certainly not disinterested! Nevertheless they are not selfish; if Heman is awaiting a miracle it is not for himself alone, but for all the dead.

Throughout his life as a musician, Heman had led the living in the praise of God. He now has a readiness to lead the dead in praise together with the living, but it belongs to God to decide the issue!

"To rise up"; the word suggests the question of resurrection, a question that was vigorously discussed at Heman's time. Some denied the resurrection (Ps 6:5), while others believed it possible (Ps 30:3). Heman makes no pronouncement on the issue, but prefers that God himself do so. Just one word on this subject and Heman will be satisfied.

Pause _____

A new pause and a new silence; what will take place in this silence?

When we are quiet after asking questions it is because we eagerly anticipate that the dialogue continue, be pursued. Heman asks some questions and then is quiet; he enters into silence so that God may break his. His desire is that the discussion with God go on, and that God be as involved in the discussion as he is and with same passion. Heman longs for God to give of himself as he is doing; that is, completely.

When Heman becomes silent, God responds to the silence with silence in return. Is this a surprise? A disappointment? A new revelation? What does God's silence mean, given that questions have been asked and his answer is expected?

Heman will very shortly speak again without any indication of disappointment or displeasure with God. What did he understand from God in God's persistent silence? What did he perceive that meant not ceasing to pray in full confidence and with love?

You know, reader friend, that Elijah heard the sound of God's silence, and that he then wrapped his face in his cloak because God so gave of himself in the silence (1 Kgs 19: 12–13). Does Heman also enter the depth of God's silence?

Heman is quiet; his silence is open to God and to him alone since he alone is present, and he alone can fill Heman's silence. Heman listens in silence to God's silence. The absence of his friends is no trouble; on the contrary, it leaves the field free for his lone discussion with God. Any friends might have interrupted the silence, thoughtlessly intervening, speaking in God's place, obstructing God's communication with Heman.

What should we now say about the absence of friends? What good could they do? Isn't involvement with God enough at a moment as important as death? If God has removed his friends, why has he done this? Heman begins to understand that in his love God wishes to be alone with him. God's silence begins to speak.

Heman knows that God has made his grave; he remembers that he had done the same for Moses, and that he had made sure to be alone to bury him. This had taken place without any witness, in God's great, exclusive intimacy; Heman finds that the same is happening with him.

"You have removed my friends far from me"; suddenly this statement no longer contains any hint of reproach and wonder takes its place. God has taken away his friends at the moment of Heman's death in favor of a greater and deeper intimacy.

Heman's silence is plunged into the silence of intimacy with God.

I believe that Heman has discovered the silence to be the response and indeed the most beautiful response he could receive, as full as it is of love. In the silence, Heman perceives what can only be perceived in silence—God's feelings.

God's feelings! Indeed, a God who is moved; here we have a real revelation. Silence is needed to enter God's heart; the silence of intimacy is needed to discover how God feels. We are not talking about just any emotion, but the feelings of a friend burying a friend; emotion like this is deep enough only to be revealed in silence. Neither is it just any silence, but rather the silence that follows the rending of a garment in mourning, when no more words come from a throat choked with sorrow. Heman is plunged into the silence of God. The questions he has asked fall into the silence and find their only answer in God's emotion . . . an infinite love that gives the silence the savor of eternity, the savor of God's tenderness.

Heman has tasted in the silence the tenderness of the one who laid him in the tomb; an infinite silence that nothing can disturb.

Heman speaks again, perhaps when the intensity of God's silence is too much for him. God's feelings can pick us up and carry us, but there comes a moment when we must embrace and carry them. It is difficult to bear God's feelings.[5]

Heman speaks again; perhaps he considers that he may have caused God pain with his clumsy questions. He will ask some new questions which will enlarge the horizon so that others may taste what

---

5. The word here in French is consistently *emotion*. Emotion is too clinical in English; "feelings" perhaps is too simple, but the idea is the strong feeling in God's heart. (Trans.)

he has tasted. These are questions that don't expect any answers, which Heman drops into the silence of the closest of friends.

Heman speaks again without awaiting any answer; God's silence has given the most beautiful of replies.

Will your faithfulness be proclaimed . . .

"Will your faithfulness be proclaimed in the tomb? Your truth in the kingdom of death? Will your miracles be known in the darkness? And your justice in the land where all is forgotten?" In this series of questions there is no trace of reproach or the least demand for God to justify himself. Each question brings forward a positive trait of God's, his faithfulness, his truth, his miracles, and his justice.

The passive voice is used in each phrase, demonstrating Heman's one concern, the one thing that has his attention, that God be preached among the dead. Who will go down into hell to proclaim God's wonders? One preacher or many? Heman does not specify, but there would need only to be one to fill him with joy. The essential thing is that one person at least be perfectly free among the dead to announce the greatness of God. Who then? You and I know the response very well, reader friend! But Heman is not waiting for a reply; he has no wish to force God's silence. He leaves the questions in suspense to return to his discussion with the God of his salvation, the God whose name is always on his lips.

As for me, **Lord**, I implore your help

After this series of questions, which show that Heman's horizon is enlarged to take in all the dead together, his prayer cannot be understood as selfish. It is not for himself alone that Heman implores God's help, but for all those who, with him, are laid in the depths of the pit. A heart that has tasted God's love cannot be closed in on itself. If, still, no one is preaching among the dead, Heman prays in their midst, for them, "LORD, I implore your help."

No one had yet preached among the dead and neither does Heman, but this does not mean that he does not pronounce the unspeakable name, the name of the living God who gives life. In this fact he is already preaching; he says what has never previously been said in the darkness of death, "LORD."

In the morning my prayer will come before you

This is quite extraordinary. Heman is in the heart of the night, a night that will perhaps know no morning since it is the night of the place of the dead, and here he evokes as a certitude the morning. The use of the future in this man's mouth is wonderful with hope. The night of the tomb will have a morning! A wonderful morning, which will see Heman's prayer rise up towards God.

Heman chooses his words; it is the musician of the Jerusalem temple who is speaking here. The words "come before" mean exactly "arise in the east." The musician would always stand in the east of the temple; Heman's prayer will arise like the sun, in the glory of a new morning . . . The night of the tomb is overturned, swept away by a dawn that will serve as the backdrop to the musician's prayer. God is already silent to receive this prayer of light.

It is a wonderful hope, full of secret exultation.

But the night is still there. It still has some difficult questions to drag out of Heman, questions that God alone can answer should he break his silence and reply.

Supplication retakes the upper hand and suddenly invades the exultation.

The Psalm of Descent into Hell

Why, **Lord**, do you reject my soul? _____

There is an unspeakable suffering in these words.

The Hebrew word translated as "reject" or "push away" has a connotation of a stink or stench. Heman has found that he is repugnant to his friends; will it prove the same for his last friend? If his body has nauseated his friends, will his soul prove sickening to the one who was not afraid to lay his friend in the tomb?

Heman feels that a distance is coming between himself and God, not because he is moving away from God but because God himself is pushing away his soul . . . an immeasurable pain!

If death brings the corruption of the body, must it also corrupt the soul? Heman doesn't know; sorrow grabs a hold of him and drags the question out of him, "Why, Lord, do you reject my soul?"

Heman attaches himself once more to the only name he knows to invoke, still counting himself pure enough to pronounce it, "Lord."

But God does not reply. Heman, moreover, does not give him time to do so. Perhaps he is afraid of what the answer might bring, fear of being unable to bear it . . .

Heman continues . . .

Why do you hide your face from me? _____

The God to whom Heman speaks is not one who is absent or distant; everything in the psalm speaks of God's proximity. The proximity is so great that it allows Heman to note the slightest of his friend's movements. Just one move away and immediately Heman knows it and wonders if it is to do with the stench of sin in his soul.

God has turned his face away, to hide himself from Heman. The musician's eyes may be failing but he still sees enough to sense this new, silent gesture of God.

"Why do you hide your face from me?"

God does hide his face from people's sin (Ps 51:9), and there is no doubt that sin makes the soul repugnant to God. This may well be true, but sinner or not, Heman is neither more nor less so now than he was before, and it hadn't prevented God from drawing near for his burial. In his love God has put to the side the issue of sin. Why would he suddenly turn his face away after he has laid his friend in the tomb.

God at no point replies! Could he do so? What does a close friend do after laying his companion in the ground? What does he do beside turn his face sadly away? And why?

Don't ask this question, Heman! God will not answer, quite simply because he is weeping . . . He turns away his face to hide the silent tears that he lets fall in secret.

Heman doesn't await God's answer to his question; no doubt he had understood. How often he had sung in the temple a verse he knew well; "precious in the sight of the LORD is the death of his saints" (Ps 116:15).

I am overwhelmed . . . my companion is darkness

Heman rallies what strength remains to speak of what is crushing him, this overpowering which comes from God, as if God himself was laying all his weight upon him.

Is this expression of being "overwhelmed" adequate to describe Heman's experience? Surely not. The word translated as "overwhelm" can also refer to humility. Heman is supporting the full weight of God's humility.

Heman has so much trouble describing his experience that he gives a number of details, each of them similar to the others.

Heman feels it all to be a form of "anger" that God batters him with! But is it really anger as we understand it? To speak of it, Heman uses a word that is only used in reference to God. Indeed it is used in the plural to give added intensity, and this is the only time anywhere in the Bible. This "anger" resembles nothing that can be seen among people. The Hebrew word designates, properly speaking, the heat issuing from the nostrils,[6] as if Heman can feel the intense heat from God's nostrils! (The word translated "terrors" in the next line is also one reserved for God alone.)

The description Heman gives of his last moments suggests an embrace from God who "encircles" him and "closes in on him." Heman is at his end . . . and God wishes to "bring him to silence."

In this silence Heman becomes one with the one who envelops him in his silence, as he wraps himself in darkness (Ps 18:12).

Heman feels as if he is drowning, as he senses nothing but God's tears!

Heman sinks into this infinite embrace, saying with his last breath and in the breath from God's nostrils, "My companion is the darkness."

For the Saturday of resurrection eve

I bless God for this psalm; the prayer is a real treasure, a miracle of faith which I receive with wonderment and thankfulness. It creates in us a thirst for a similar closeness with God; it awakens in us a deep compassion for the dying; it prepares us for the day of our own death. Without actually anticipating that day, we can pray that the psalm fashion our heart and prepare us for this great moment. The psalm no doubt passes our limited faith, but in his grace God can strengthen our faith by his Holy Spirit through these words. What will the day of my death be? Of course I don't know, but I ask God that he might be as close to me as he was Heman, and that he be so from now, so that I not be found wanting in my final hour.

To whom should we turn to teach us to pray this psalm in its profound truth and to live it out fully. Who, after Heman, was able to live it and so teach it?

---

6. See for example 2 Sam 22:9; "there went out a smoke from his nostrils."

I can't see anyone other than Christ himself. Like every good Israelite, Jesus prayed all the psalms, including this one. He would have prayed it many times in his life, following the practice of the Jewish liturgy. He appropriated it and was impregnated with it to the point that in his death he begins to resemble what is described here; indeed Heman in some way prefigures Christ. To read this psalm on the Saturday of Holy Week, in the great silence of that day, is to enter into the depth of the psalm, as also the depth of the mystery of Christ's death. More than Heman, it is Jesus whom we hear pronouncing this prayer. So, I marvel again and bless God still more for this prayer.

We need to go through the psalm again, verse by verse, hearing it as in the mouth of the Crucified. It then becomes clear with a new light, in a gripping way. At the same time, the psalm illuminates the cross, the laying of Christ in the tomb, the descent into hell, underlining all their spiritual density and profundity.

All the church fathers understood this psalm as from the mouth of Christ. They underscore the fact that Jesus cried out from the cross, even as the darkness invaded the land in fullness of day; and the fact that this darkness which was Christ's companion was the same darkness in which God wraps himself when he draws near to people, as stated in another psalm (18:11). The fathers were particularly given to emphasize how Christ alone could say in truth, more so than Heman, that he was "free among the dead," since he alone had no debt to pay death.

Christ is the answer so much awaited by Heman to his questions. Christ is God's answer, the "yes" of God to the two first questions, "Will you do miracles for the dead? Will the dead rise up to give you praise?" Jesus embodies the "yes" of God, since he is the one who descended into the grave to proclaim his faithfulness, his truth, and his justice.

At the end of each prayer, an Amen is pronounced by whoever acknowledges its truth and sees himself in it; at the end of Heman's Psalm, comes Christ, God's silent Amen.

— CHAPTER 3 —

Christ and Mary Magdalene

1 On the first day of the week, Mary Magdalene came early in the morning to the tomb when it was still dark, and she saw that the stone had been rolled away from the sepulcher. 2 She ran and came to where Simon Peter was, with the other disciple, whom Jesus loved, and told them, "They have taken away the Lord from the tomb and we don't know where they have put him."

3 So Peter and the other disciple went out and made their way to the tomb. 4 The two ran together but the other disciple ran more quickly than Peter and came to the tomb first. 5 Bending down, he saw the linen wrappings lying on the ground but did not go in. 6 Then Simon Peter, following him, arrived, went into the tomb and saw the wrappings on the ground 7 and the cloth that had been placed over his face, not with the rest of the bandaging but folded in a place apart. 8 Then the other disciple, who had arrived first at the tomb, entered; he saw and he believed. 9 He had not previously understood the Scriptures according to which he must be raised from the dead. 10 Then the disciples went back to where they were staying.

11 Mary stayed outside, near the tomb, weeping. As she was weeping she bent down towards the tomb 12 and she saw two angels clothed in white, sitting where the body of Jesus had been laid, one at the head and the other at the feet. 13 They said to her, "Woman, why are you weeping?" She answered them, "Because they have taken away my Lord, and I don't know where they have laid him." 14 When she had said this, she turned around and she saw Jesus standing there, but she didn't know it was Jesus. 15 Jesus said to her, "Woman, why are you weeping? Who are you looking for?" She, thinking it was the gardener, said to him, "Sir, if it is you who have taken him away, tell me where you have laid him and I will go and remove him." 16 Jesus said to her, "Mary!" She turned back and said in Hebrew, "Rabboni," which is to say, "Master." 17 Jesus said to her, "Don't touch me, because I am not yet ascended to the Father. But go to my brothers and tell them that I am going to my Father and your Father, to my God and your God."

18 Then Mary Magdalene went to tell his disciples, "I have seen the Lord, and this is what he said to me." (John 20)

No one was a witness to the moment when Jesus was raised from among the dead. Once resurrected, he appeared to many, but no one was present at his resurrection. Christ's death took place before a whole crowd, but the resurrection took place in the secret place of God; it belongs to the intimacy of God. The resurrection is hidden in the night as a secret of the Father's love for the Son in the Holy Spirit. Even running, as did Peter and John, we will always arrive too late; the tomb is already empty. Even in Paradise, we will not be there for the resurrection; Christ will be there, alive, eternally alive, with a life whose mystery is beyond us, the life of God.

Indeed, the resurrection of Christ pertains to the intimate presence of God. The death of the Crucified One[1] has this intimacy as its very language, an intimacy in which wounding was deeply felt; but the resurrection is the very life of God, a life whose mystery is greater yet than that of the cross. The resurrection belongs to the inexpressible depths of intimacy between the Father, the Son, and the Holy Spirit. Human words do not allow us to speak of the depths of divine love, which indeed is too much for our understanding. The resurrection is an attestation, a manifestation of this indestructible divine life, against

---

1. The author consistently prefers not to capitalize "the crucified" and "the crucified one," stressing Jesus' humanity. However, in translation we have followed the normal English-language practice of capitalizing. (Trans.)

which Satan has not the least hold. Satan had been stealthily present near the cross, but he is absolutely nowhere on Easter morning. In the ineffable clarity of paschal light, Satan can cast no shadow since he is definitively absent. He had been "cast out," to use Jesus own expression (John 12:31); he has totally disappeared. Indeed, it is incongruous to even speak of him, to such a degree is the thought of his name effaced by the resurrection.

Given that the Bible is silent about the actual moment of resurrection and speaks only of different encounters with Jesus as resurrected, we need to do the same. So, without risking a more lengthy dissertation on the resurrection, I prefer to restrict myself to discussing one single encounter with the Risen Jesus; not all of them, since I am not up to it and it would take too long; just the first. So, with God's help, we will look at the encounter between Mary Magdalene and Jesus as it is recorded in John's Gospel; this is the Gospel in which the encounter is most fully developed and so, no doubt, the easiest on which to comment.

The women on Easter morning

How many women were there on that morning in the garden of the tomb? How many were present when they found the tomb empty? It is impossible to say. Matthew reports that there were two (Mary Magdalene and the other Mary, 28:1). Mark speaks of three women (Mary Magdalene, Mary the mother of James, and Salome, 16:1) and Luke still more (Mary Magdalene, Joanna, Mary, and others, 24:10). The Gospels do not agree on the number, but they all mention the presence of Mary Magdalene and all name her first. She is, *par excellence*, the one who met the resurrected Jesus.

John is well aware that in accordance with the Old Testament two or three witnesses were needed to validate something as fact (see Deut 19:15). So, in passing on the testimony of one woman alone, John makes no endeavor to present the resurrection as an event that could be the object of legal witness. His desire is rather to show that an encounter with the risen Christ is beyond any attempt aimed at providing a proof of its reality. Perception of the resurrection is not communicable, far beyond pinning down. A person who encounters the Risen One is convinced of the reality of his experience, but he also knows that it is not an event for a court of law.

John gives us the impression that Mary had gone to the tomb alone, although he knew very well that this was not the case. Mary was not in fact alone, as we realize when she says to the disciples, *"We* don't know where they have laid him" (20:2). This "we" in Mary's mouth clearly shows that she was not alone in front of the open tomb. Nevertheless, the remainder of the account emphasizes Mary's aloneness; there is no further allusion to the others. With the angels she no longer says "we don't know," but rather "I don't know." With Jesus, after this, Mary appears in definite solitude.

This peculiarity of the story as given by John—who was not unaware of the presence of the other women, but nonetheless substantially ignores them—is a way of presenting Mary in her inner solitude. Even if the other women are there, Mary is alone within herself. It is in the deepest place of this inner solitude that Jesus meets with her, where no one other than God can meet with us. John intends to show us that for us too it is in the deepest place of the heart that the Risen One comes to meet us, this growing intimacy little by little transforming our inner solitude.

Mary's tears

Once the two disciples had left (v. 10) the interest is Mary's tears (v. 11). No doubt she had wept before, but John waits for the disciples' departure before speaking of her tears, making sure they are seen as tears of solitude. This woman weeps without witness; she weeps in the depths of her solitude. The more one suffers, the more alone one feels, even if there are others around. Standing in front of the empty tomb, Mary feels infinitely alone and weeps to the measure of her solitude. John underlines the importance of these tears by using the word "weep" four times (vv. 11 [x 2], 13, 15). The first thing the angels notice, and Jesus too, is Mary's tears.

It was the custom for the women to gather to weep together over a death, and that they lament in public; this was part of the ritual of mourning. The lamentations of the weeping women spoke of their fellowship in mourning. Here we are dealing with something quite different; Mary is alone to weep; she has waited to be alone and remains alone. Her tears are not ritual; they can be shared with no one because her pain is too deep to be shared. The depth of mourning reveals the depth of her attachment to Christ. Only the angels and Jesus himself could be witnesses of such tears. They alone try to meet Mary in her tears; "Why do you weep?" they say to her.

When a woman stands weeping in front of a tomb it is hardly necessary to ask this sort of question! Everybody knows that death causes tears to fall. The question can be asked here though, because there is more to it; Mary's tears are more than just those of mourning. Her suffering is double; not only, indeed, does she weep the death of one who was dear to her, but also the body of the one she laments has disappeared from the tomb. There is no funeral rite for such a sad situation; "They have taken away my Lord and I know not where they have laid him!"

The angels have no time to console Mary because she immediately turns away. Jesus has drawn near. He meets her in her pain; "Woman, why are you weeping?" It is her distress to which he is attentive, the loneliness of this woman, her wounded love which has no way to be expressed other than through tears. Jesus draws near and is concerned for this love in distress; "Woman, why do you weep?"

Mary Magdalene

Who exactly is this woman? From Matthew's Gospel we know that she had followed Jesus from Galilee (27:55–56), and that she was part of his inmost circle, alongside the disciples. We could spend longer on what is said in the other Gospels but I prefer not to because it is rather complex; the number of women named Mary means there has been much confusion about them from the time of the first commentaries of the church fathers, so I prefer to stay just with what is said in John's Gospel; this avoids complicating our understanding of what took place in her encounter with the Risen One, early on Easter morning.

The first time John speaks of Mary Magdalene is in 19:25, where he mentions her presence at the foot of the cross, among those closest to Jesus: "Near the cross stood his mother and his mother's sister, Mary the wife of Clopas, and Mary Magdalene."

"Near the cross"; she had therefore experienced the death of Jesus at very close quarters, right up to his final breath. She had also been present during everything that followed, until, indeed, he was laid in the tomb. Already close and an intimate of Jesus, she became even more so during the intense hours spent at the foot of the cross.

The three "visions"

Mary's meeting with the Risen One on Easter morning is not the only encounter she had that day; it is preceded by two others, with the two disciples to whom she went bearing news, and with the angels. In this succession of encounters a progression in intensity and profundity becomes apparent. This progression is plain in each of the things she sees ("visions")[2] which introduce these encounters.

It all begins with the fact that Mary "sees" that the stone on the tomb has been taken away (v. 1). John describes this sight using the

---

2. The French word used. (Trans.)

simple word "to see" (*blepō*), thereby fixing her vision at the simple level of ordinary, physical sight. What Mary saw would perhaps have been seen by anyone; moreover, Mary is at pains to seek out the disciples so that they too can see what she saw: the stone had been taken away from the entrance to the tomb.

Immediately after the departure of the disciples, Mary sees something else, two angels. On this occasion, to describe what she sees, John uses a different Greek word (*theōreō*), which locates Mary's vision at a different level of depth and intensity.

According to the etymology current at John's time, the verb *theōreō* means to see like God (*theos*) sees (*oraō*), to see as God may enable us to see. This is particularly so as it concerns the angels; these are not visible except to God and those whom God enables to see. Mary, then, sees the angels, perhaps with her physical eyes, but above all with the eyes of her heart, with all the intensity and depth of inward sight received from God.

Today this ancient etymology is not retained by specialists, but this is not so important. To understand John and not to go against what he writes, we need to hold to the etymology current at his time. If Mary sees angels, it is because God has opened her eyes (cf. Num 22:31), which is to say the eyes of her heart, rather than her physical eyes. Mary is well aware of experiencing something exceptional, and that what she is seeing, perhaps, would not be seen by the disciples. In as much as she had gone in search of them to tell them the stone had been taken away, so now she avoids searching the disciples out to tell them of the angels' presence! She doesn't go to tell anyone else and seeks no other witness . . . She doesn't even mention the angels, shortly thereafter, to the disciples (v. 18).

Finally, John tells us, Mary "sees" Jesus (v. 14). To portray this third vision, the evangelist again uses the verb employed in connection with the angels (*theōreō*). The Risen One is also visible only to those to whom it is given of God. Mary is not concerned to find some possible further witness any more than she had with regard to the angels.

While the vision of the angels and that of the Risen One are both on a spiritual level, it is not with the same depth; the vision of the Risen One is much deeper than that of the angels. We can perceive this when we notice that the angels are described, whereas Jesus is not. The angels, John tells us, are "dressed in white" (v. 12), but no such descriptive detail is given of Jesus. It is easier to describe angels than Jesus. Mary immediately understands that she is seeing angels, though it is perhaps the first time in her life, but she does not immediately understand that she is in Jesus' presence; she manages to confuse him with the caretaker of the garden, although Jesus is much better known to her than angels! It is easier to recognize angels than the Risen One! This tells us that much more acute, profound vision is needed to see him! This is indeed true; it is a very particular gift from God that he gives Mary when she sees the Risen One. God has opened the eyes of her heart.

Where John takes time to describe the angels and not Jesus, this does not mean that Jesus is of secondary importance compared with the angels! Quite obviously, the opposite is so. It means rather that vision of the Risen Christ more nearly touches the indescribable than a vision of angels; it is closer to the vision of the one nobody can describe; vision of the resurrected Jesus is similar to vision of God. How could it be otherwise since he is God?

The same happens in the other Gospels; God's messengers on Easter morning are invariably described in terms of their external appearance (Matt 28:3; Mark 16:5; Luke 24:4), but Jesus never is. To see the Risen Lord belongs to the realm of the inexpressible; such vision is so much more profound and beyond apprehension than that of angels.

The angels can be precisely located in terms of where they appeared; "there where Jesus had been laid, one seated at the head, the other at the feet" (v. 12). When it comes to Jesus, he cannot be pinned down! John becomes increasingly brief in his way of describing the indescribable; "she saw Jesus standing" (v. 14). Where was he standing? John does not say. Some translations say "he stood there," but this is to add the adverb "there," which is not in the Greek. The presence of the Risen Jesus truly cannot be localized or described.

As can be seen, Mary's three "visions" occupy levels of perception of increasing profundity; first, the stone, on the physical level, then the angels at a spiritual level, and then the Risen Jesus much deeper still... With him it is as with God; it is not within humanity's gift to be able to localize or describe him with precision!

The close of the account leaves us with a paradoxical situation; Mary goes to tell the disciples, "I have seen the Lord" (v. 18). John now puts in Mary's mouth the verb "to see" in its more banal form (*oraō*). For Mary, her encounter with Jesus is an indisputable reality. She knows very well that she saw Christ as clearly as she saw the stone rolled away, and that is indeed the case. She had even wished to touch him. Nevertheless, when she tells her story to the disciples, Mary does not launch into any description of the one she "saw"; that would be a risk too far.

Why then use the word "see" in this common form? Not to put the encounter into the simple and banal realm of the physical, but to convey how sure she is of what she saw. The word indicates the certainty of faith, not that what she saw was somehow normal. The ambiguity remains, however, inescapable; allowed to see the indescribable, she is nonetheless so sure of what she saw that she speaks as if it were an everyday event.

This is how it always is; between the reality of spiritual experience and how we speak about it there is always room for confusion; the one who speaks of his experience does not always make it clear that it was something given him by God. The vision is so strong that the eyes of the heart and the eyes of the body become one, the human person becomes so unified in the vision of the invisible. Mary had well and truly seen the invisible. She tells the truth when she says that she "saw" the Lord, but what she doesn't say is that the vision is not of ordinary access. Because she doesn't describe him, what she says is profoundly true; in this way she keeps the inexpressible just that.

The different dialogues

Each of Mary's encounters includes an element of speech.

After seeing that the stone had been taken away, Mary goes immediately to look for the two disciples to tell them what she can. This particular snatch of speech does not become a dialogue; the disciples do not reply; they go to check for themselves what Mary has told them, but they don't say anything to her. They are silent at the tomb and return in silence. There is no dialogue.

With the angels, a real discussion is engaged at the angels' initiative, but it doesn't go very far. Mary replies to the angels' question but then suddenly turns away from them because of a mysterious presence that attracts her attention. It is then that she sees Jesus.

The dialogue with Jesus is the only one we can really describe as such. It picks up and goes over the same ground broached by the angels, and then goes further. I ask myself, reader friend, whether it is not always so. No dialogue is ever as profound as one that is conducted by Jesus. With him it is the same as with God; no one knows me as well as him; no one knows as well as he what questions to ask; I am never as free as with him; he alone knows the words that carry us forward. In our conversations with others we can never go as far as in talking with him. The depth of the exchanges cannot be compared.

The progression through the account of Easter morning is quite extraordinary; as the vision becomes deeper and more intense, so the dialogue becomes deeper and more intense.

A leitmotif

With the different people she speaks to, each time Mary begins by saying almost the same thing. In what she says to the disciples, to the angels, and to Jesus, each time the same two phrases appear.

"They have *taken away* the Lord, and we don't know where they have *laid* him." (v. 2)

"They have *taken away* my Lord, and I don't know where they have *laid* him." (v. 13)

"If it is you who has moved him, tell me where you have *laid* him and I will come and *take him away*." (v. 15)

Mary is unable to make any step forward in her thinking because she is obsessed with the body of Christ, which has been taken away and laid somewhere else. Neither the disciples nor the angels manage to help her onwards. Only Jesus lifts her out of her obsession.

Mary's obsession

The two recurring words in what Mary says are nicely chosen by John; in the other passage in the Gospel in which she appears he had used them to describe the scene she witnessed. When John mentions Mary for the first time, at the foot of the cross, he does so to stress the link there is between that day and Easter morning. The degree to which this woman was traumatized by Christ's death is made apparent. What had she seen? Of all Christ's last moments, from the whole event, she just retains two scenes, which quite literally obsess her.

Anyone who is present at the death of a loved one is forever marked by some aspect, some detail of what they see, and this becomes deeply engraved on the memory. Each of us, it seems to me, guard in our heart unforgettable details of the loved one's end, which can eventually become really obsessional. What was it, in John's words, that Mary saw at Golgotha? She saw Joseph of Arimathea "take away" the body of Jesus from the cross (19:38); then she saw the body of the Crucified "laid" in the tomb by Joseph and Nicodemus (19:42). She had indeed witnessed other scenes, but these two are described with the two verbs that form part of her obsession. The two scenes are so indelible that they have not left her and are still disturbing her when she stands in front of the empty tomb; who now had "taken away" from the tomb the one they had "taken away" from the cross? Where had they "laid" the one they had "laid" in the tomb?

The descent from the cross and the laying in the tomb; these are the scenes imprinted on Mary to the point of obsession. The strong words describing them are still in force and resurface each time she speaks, always with Christ's body in mind. She is unable to speak of anything else to those she meets; the disciples, the angels, the gardener . . .

The descent from the cross and the laying in the tomb; these two scenes both follow Christ's death. Mary does not think of anything connected with Jesus' last moments alive, which she had nevertheless witnessed. The only concern in her mind is to do with the dead body; macabre and morbid images which surge within her when she finds the body has disappeared.

Both scenes which obsess Mary have to do with the dead body being handled by those who touched it. Physical contact with the dead body, this is what obsesses Mary. She is so impressed by the image of the body that it serves as her point of reference to position the two angels; one seated where the head had lain and the other at his feet.

A corpse cannot be touched without one becoming unclean according to Jewish law (see Num 19:11). Those who had taken Christ down from the cross and had laid him in the tomb were therefore unclean. Who would have dared touch the body of the Crucified again? Mary could surely not suspect the two disciples, nor the angels, since angels do not touch corpses! By contrast, she could certainly suspect the garden caretaker since the garden in question was a cemetery, and it is quite normal for a cemetery caretaker to touch tombs or corpses. This is why she speaks so differently to the gardener compared to the angels; "If it is you who have moved him, tell me where you have laid him and I will come to take him away." Mary is so troubled that she is prepared to become unclean herself by going to take charge of the missing body.

Confronted by such distress, Jesus has a wonderful thing to say, the only thing that could free Mary from her morbid obsession; "Touch me not!"

"Don't touch me"; the body you see is not a corpse; it is alive and this life now frees you from your obsession and heals your trauma. Encounter with the Resurrected One frees us, indeed, from every morbid obsession, from being obsessed with the death of others or our own death.

She was looking for the dead, she finds the living, the Living! She would have become unclean had she touched the dead, so why should she not now touch the body of the living? Could it be because in rising from the dead the Resurrected One is still marked by the impurity of the tomb and the place of the dead? Not at all! The Resurrected One is alive with the life of the Holy God. It is the Holy One who has taken him out from among the dead. He cannot be touched because he is Holy. It is the living who are still too unclean to touch the Holy One of God. The only one who may do so is the Father, to whom he will shortly ascend. Between the Father and the Son there is a fellowship of life, the depth of which is in its holiness, the sanctity of infinite love.

The inexpressible

"Who are you looking for?" Jesus asks. Curiously, in her reply, Mary doesn't name the one she seeks. When she was speaking to the disciples she referred to Jesus as "the Lord" (v. 2); then when speaking to the angels she says a little more, "my Lord." We easily perceive the progression between "the Lord" and "my Lord'; to the angels she expresses the depth of her attachment to Christ. But this time, talking to Jesus, Mary goes still further, much deeper, suggesting the inexpressible; she designates the one she seeks by a simple pronoun, "him." "If it is you that have moved *him*, tell me where you have laid *him*, and I will come and take *him* away" (v. 15). Speaking in this way, Mary speaks of Jesus in the way God was spoken of, without pronouncing his name, belonging as it does to the ineffable.

At no point in the account does Mary pronounce Jesus' name . . . When she rejoins the disciples she says simply that she has seen "the Lord." What exactly does she intend by this expression? Does she speak of Jesus as one speaks of God, as the one true "Lord"? Or does she rather speak of him as a disciple speaks of their human master? I believe she speaks at once both of the humanity and divinity of the one who appeared to her in the garden of the tomb.

"Mary," he said

Mary saw that the stone had been rolled away; she saw that the body was no longer in the tomb; she saw the angels; but in all of this she failed to perceive any sign of God, no miracle. No sign or miracle was enough to convince her of the resurrection. With the gardener she is still bewailing the one she consistently considered dead. Angels were seated at the exact site of the corpse; they were there to comfort and endeavored to do so, but in vain; she was inconsolable over Christ's death and the disappearance of his body.

No sign and no miracle, not even the appearance of angels could convince Mary of the resurrection! By contrast, one word pronounced by the gardener was enough and she was plunged deep into the mystery of God; "Mary!" With this word she knew the Risen One, the Living One; not a word of explanatory apologetic, not a word of argumentation or reason, but a simple word that, in Jesus' mouth, decisively speaks into being a personal encounter; "Mary!"

It was in a familiar gesture, that of breaking bread, that Jesus made himself known to the disciples at Emmaus. It is in a name, the most familiar possible, that he makes himself known here. Although

Mary's eyes had been open she had been unable to discern Jesus in the supposed gardener. Her ears too, though open, were unable to discern the voice of Jesus. Mary's heart was not yet open. By pronouncing Mary's name, Jesus takes away the stone that obstructed the heart of this woman. It is at the deepest level of the heart that the Risen One communed with her; it is here that he communes with us too. To the degree to which the heart is closed, to that degree it is not possible to take hold of the mystery of Christ's resurrection. The Risen One opens Mary's heart to this mystery by the power of his word.

"Woman," Jesus had said. The force of this word was not sufficient to open Mary's heart. "Mary," Christ now says. It's in proceeding down the road of intimacy that Jesus' word takes on its full force.

Shocked at hearing her name, Mary is altogether overcome. She discovers that he who was dead is alive. There could be no greater turning upside down, no greater revolution than this. A whole succession of words in the account tell the depth of this reversal and all in just one verse (v. 16); 1) Mary turns, 2) she breaks into Hebrew, 3) she becomes suddenly silent after just the one word, 4) she seeks to touch Jesus.

The overwhelming turnaround in Mary is as great as the rolling away of a tombstone. With regard to this avalanche of feeling Jesus will need to take fresh steps; but first we will pause over the change itself.

She turns

When her name is spoken, John tells us, Mary "turned" (v. 16), as if her name had been spoken to her back, when that surely isn't so since Mary had already turned to be facing him. How curious!

We need to read the text carefully. Mary had already turned once to speak to Jesus as she was speaking to the angels: "saying this [to the angels], she turned and saw Jesus standing there . . ." (v. 14). What a strange account this is; Mary interrupts her conversation with the angels and turns to face Jesus, then she turns round again when Jesus calls her by her name, again to face him. What can John wish to say through this duplicated action? What is really going on?

The double turning of Mary to face Jesus certainly isn't a physical turning, a movement of the body, but rather an interior one, a spiritual about-face. The encounter with the Risen One is experienced in the depths of the heart, as we have already noted. When the Risen One speaks to us, his word provokes multiple, successive turnings within us! The voice of the Risen One surges forth in such a way that it always causes us to turn and respond. His word catches us off balance and turns us around within.

Are these interior revolutions of the same order as conversion? Without doubt, yes! In fact, it is with the same verb "to turn" (*strephō*, not the classical Greek *epistrephō*) that John renders the idea of conversion (see 12:40). The great change caused by the meeting with the Risen One is a profound conversion.

So, Mary's first movement to turn away from the angels could not be construed as merely physical; indeed, in the presence of an angel it is unallowable, inconceivable even, that one would turn away. Rather, one is prostrated, that is if not transfixed by fear; to turn one's back on an angel is simply not done, least of all to speak to a gardener! Who could this gardener have been to have such an impact on Mary before he even opens his mouth or makes a sound to indicate his presence? The power of the silent presence of the Risen One is such that Mary interrupts her dialogue with the angel and turns her back on them!

The Risen One has the same effect in our lives; the perception of his silent presence is enough to turn us around internally. His presence is perceptible; it is felt, but without it being possible to say quite how. Mary, then, turns without even being able to recognize the one who affects her still more than the angels!

She was turned around

In verse 14, as in verse 16, the verb used by John is employed in a passive form, the sense of which is both passive and reflexive; it can be translated equally by "she turned round" or "she was turned around"; the Greek says both.

Certainly, Mary herself turned round, firstly because she sensed the presence of the Risen One, then when she heard her name. But to say this is not enough. Of himself, man lacks the power necessary to be converted, to turn to the Risen Christ. On his own, man is unable to turn to God; it happens only if God enables him, so it is appropriate that our text suggests that "Mary was turned." Turned by whom? We have here a fine example of the "divine passive" as it is termed by grammarians, signifying that God is the logical subject of the verb.

Mary "was turned" in the first place by the only one whose silent presence is more powerful than the words of angels; and secondly, by the one who alone by simply speaking a name can reach into the depths of the heart.

Mary's interior turnings are not just her own actions; above all they are a work of Christ who, as much by his silence as by his word, can turn a life round. There is a divine/human synergy in this profound internal alteration, this conversion.

No doubt we can add that the cohesive force of this synergy is provided by the Holy Spirit. Who is there, indeed, other than him, who can enable us to perceive the silent presence of the Risen One in our lives—not if he has himself done nothing to bring us to this recognition? Who other than the Holy Spirit can direct our lives towards him who manifests himself to us so mysteriously? Of himself, without the help of the Holy Spirit, man is absolutely incapable of discerning the silent presence of the Risen One. When Christ draws us to himself, either in silence or by word, the Holy Spirit is also there impelling us towards him. Our interior revolution, our conversion, is also the work of the Holy Spirit, working together with the power of the word and of the silence of Christ.

She speaks to him in Hebrew

The change in Mary is such that she starts to speak in the sacred language, language used only in holy places and certainly not in a cemetery. She breaks into the language of those few who have the right of speech in the sanctuary, which is to say men and not women. What an alteration in Mary!

She speaks in the sacred language, which is to say, the language of prayer. The use of Hebrew was confined to reading the Bible, the holy book, and liturgical prayer. Bible commentaries were not in Hebrew but in Aramaic.

If John considers it appropriate here to specify that Mary is speaking Hebrew, it's because he wishes to draw our attention to the fact that she is praying. What she says to Jesus is a prayer, just as one would pray to God in the temple or a synagogue. This is the only time in the Gospels where it is specified that someone speaks to Jesus in the Hebrew. What could this mean except that Mary knows that being in the presence of the Risen One is to be in the presence of God? He alone is able to cause prayer to flow from the depths of our disorientated hearts.

When the Risen One calls her by name, Mary, then, responds with prayer . . .

Rabbouni

Rabbouni is a Hebrew word and Rabbi is Aramaic. In John's Gospel Jesus is frequently called Rabbi (1:38, 49; 3:2; 4:31; 6:25; 9:2; 11:8), as indeed was John the Baptist (3:26).

It was in this way, in Aramaic, that spiritual leaders were addressed, and it was a title of courtesy. For the first time, in this same Gospel, someone addresses Jesus as Rabbouni. No one else is referred to in this way. What then is the difference between Rabbi and Rabbouni?

On the occasion of the first use of Rabbi, John gives the Greek translation, "Master" (1:38). In the continuation, there is no repeating of the translation when the word is used again, but when the word Rabbouni is used, he repeats the translation, "Master." John has difficulty expressing in Greek the shade of meaning there is between the two words. Rabbouni is an amplification of Rabbi with the addition of the emphatic "*nun*"; which is to say, there is a greater emphasis in Rabbouni than in Rabbi. In Mary's eyes Jesus is therefore more than a simple Rabbi.

The emphasis is increased by that fact that Rabbouni is spoken in the sacred language that was used to address God in prayer. The augmentative form, Rabbouni, implies the deference that is due to God alone. I believe indeed that Mary considers Jesus to be God.

What I am saying would certainly be more evident if the word Rabbouni appeared in the Old Testament, but this is not the case. Rabbouni ought to be a term reserved for God, but there is no attestation to this.

The only other use of Rabbouni in the New Testament is in Mark 10:51. This is also addressed to Jesus and on this occasion is found in the mouth of a blind man, Bartimaeus, where it is difficult to know quite what significance this had for him. Nevertheless, we can note at the outset of his encounter with Jesus that Bartimaeus calls him "Son of David" (10:47), a messianic title; he then calls him, "Son of David" (10:48) again, but more forcefully; and finally he calls him "Rabbouni," at the moment he addresses to him what is a real prayer, "That I may receive my sight." To whom, other than God, would Bartimaeus address such a request?

Mary was silent

After saying Rabbouni, using the sacred tongue, Mary is silent. She says nothing more and goes no further in her prayer. What else could she say? It was God standing before her! She is face to face with the inexpressible. The sacred language alone is appropriate to speak to him; only silence will do when the movement[3] of the heart is beyond speech; holy silence, that of contemplation and adoration.

The one standing before Mary had been dead; he was alive! He had been taken away from the cross and laid in the tomb; but now he is standing there in the garden alive with that indescribable life that has conquered death. The mystery of his life is beyond any words. Only silence can accompany her wonderment, not the silence of failing words but a silence beyond words, beyond sacred language, beyond God's own language, the inexpressible silence where God dwells.

In the word Rabbouni, Mary has expressed all of her love for Christ. Her silence goes further, expressing the love beyond love, inexpressible love.

Touch me not

In her silence Mary attempts a gesture that Jesus prevents; "touch me not." Mary wished to touch the Risen One even as she recognizes his divinity. How inconsistent this is, almost foolish! One does not touch God! Nevertheless this is not folly; her gesture simply shows that while realizing his divinity she also knows that he is a man and there is no blasphemy in reaching out to a person.

Christ, both God and man; this is what Mary believes and it explains her attitude and the great internal change. Mary knows what the

---

3. Here and in what follows the author uses the word *élan*, a word not used elsewhere in the book. It has no real cognate in English; it includes the ideas of movement, spirit, enthusiasm, passion, spontaneity, and has been variously translated here. (Trans.)

theologians and councils would take an age to formulate, that Jesus is perfect God and perfect man. Such is the mystery Mary finds herself before in the garden of the sepulcher . . .

What then is the action Mary attempted? What is the action appropriate to such a great mystery, an action that would respect and honor the divine humanity of Christ? John doesn't describe what Mary wished to do, but happily for us it is described in another Gospel. In the parallel account in Matthew, in fact, the women "took hold of Jesus feet and worshipped him" (28:9). It is therefore very sure that this is what Mary would have wished to do; to take hold of Jesus' feet and worship him. This would have been a silent action, adding to the silence what words were unable to say. To take hold of Jesus' feet recognizes his humanity; to adore him is to acknowledge that he is God. Mary's silent act is one of contemplative love.

Before the angels, Mary did not bow down to adore, and she was right; God alone is to be adored, not angels (see Rev 22:8, 9). Before Jesus, she intends a gesture she knows is reserved for God alone. She is well aware that there is more to Christ than an angel.

Nevertheless Jesus stops Mary in her spontaneous response. Is it that he is refusing worship as Peter would refuse to be worshipped by Cornelius (Acts 10:26)? I think not; Jesus never stopped anyone from offering him worship. Here the reason for stopping her is different, and moreover is stated to Mary: "Touch me not, because I have not yet ascended to my Father." Mary's gesture must not hold back Jesus' movement towards the Father.

"Touch me not!" A few days later Jesus would say just the opposite to Thomas, inviting him to touch both his hands and his side (20:27). In this apparent contradiction, Jesus' teaching skill is apparent. Christ, in fact, responds in accordance with the needs of the person he is speaking to, to help them progress along the way of faith; Mary needs to be held back in her wonderment, Thomas to be knocked out of his unbelief.

"I am not yet ascended to my Father." Jesus is not the goal of his worshipers' spiritual advancement; he is the way that leads to the Father. Jesus does not wish to be at the center of our contemplation. He prefers to humbly efface himself before the Father towards whom he himself reaches. He leads to the Father; the humble Jesus seeks just one thing, the glory of his Father.

The Spirit had caused Mary to turn to the Son; the Son now directs her towards the Father. The flow of love in Mary is to be relocated into the flow of love that circulates at the heart of the Trinity.

Contemplation of the Risen One is not static; it is to enter a movement, a dynamic, a flow of love that originates and comes to fulfillment in God. Mary must not stop Christ in his movement towards the Father, but must rather enter into that flow; this is worship, a flow of love wrapped up in the endlessly reciprocated love within the Trinity.

To take hold of Christ's feet, to be prostrated, to worship him . . . Jesus prevents Mary from doing what would fix her in immobility. Physical closeness is no more than a prelude to the closeness of spiritual communion. To establish this kind communion it is necessary that Christ go to his Father. "It is expedient for you that I go away," he said to his disciples (16:7). In fact, as long as Jesus is physically present in the garden of the tomb, he cannot be present as he desires to be present to each disciple, which is to say, present in the deepest place of the heart, with that presence that causes him to say that he is in us and we in him, just as he is in the Father and the Father in him (17:22–23).

The Son is in the Father and the Father in the Son; such is the immense fellowship of love, a fellowship that is not static but which the church fathers signified by a word borrowed from the world of dance, *perichōrēsē*. We are speaking here of a communion woven in perpetual movement, perpetual self-effacement, allowing each to give place to the other, like a round in which each dancer gives way to the other. So it is that the Father is in the Son and the Son in the Father. The Son leaves the tomb and ascends in grace towards the Father in order to glorify him; while the Father, drawing the Son forth from the tomb, effaces himself before him, to glorify him.

Mary's vocation

After describing the profound revolution within Mary, the text also describes her vocation, her call. This account, in fact, is similar in every respect to other biblical accounts of a calling; it has all the characteristics. On the foundation of this woman's internal revolution, Jesus has more to build and will make of her an apostle,[4] the apostle to the apostles, as the fathers admirably term her. The calling of an apostle; for Mary this is the start of a new life. Just as Jesus came out of the tomb alive, Mary will come out of the garden of the sepulcher to lead a new life. The resurrection of Christ introduces her to a new life, as she too had been resuscitated, healed of her morbid obsession.

In the biblical perspective, an account of a calling, a commission, is marked by the giving of a sign which calls attention to the special presence of God. Thus, Moses sees a bush that burns without being consumed (Exod 3:2). The temple in Jerusalem is filled with smoke when Isaiah discovers God's presence (Isa 6:4). Here, Mary's attention is caught by the tombstone that has been rolled away.

In these accounts of calling, angels often appear, as in the case of the burning bush with Moses (Exod 3:2); or indeed other celestial beings, as with the seraphim at the calling of Isaiah (6.2). The angels are not there for their own benefit; they are always there as intermediaries to direct attention to God. Beyond the angel, it is always God who is central. The seraphim sing before Isaiah, but it is God who is the focus. The angel of the burning bush very quickly retreats into the background before God, who takes over, so that we don't even know what becomes of the angel. With Mary, things are just the same; the angels prepare the dialogue with Christ and introduce him, without

---

4. A sent one. (Trans.)

our ever knowing what becomes of them during Mary's talk with Jesus. Are they still there or not? To tell the truth, it matters little; they fulfill their role in preparing a place for Jesus; they had no interest in anything other than preparing the way for Jesus. They disappear without disappearing.

In such an account of a calling, the one called is often called by name, named indeed by God himself, as can be seen for example in the account of Moses' commission: "God called to him out the midst of the bush and said to him, 'Moses, Moses'" (Exod 3:4). At the heart of the encounter with the Risen One, the mention of Mary's name is essential.

What happens next is that the one called wishes to press forward so as better to examine and engage with the mystery he sees. Moses before the burning bush intended to draw nearer, but his enthusiasm was arrested by God (Exod 3:5). The situation is very similar to that of Mary, pulled up short in her intent response by Jesus; "touch me not" because the fire within me will burn you.

The commission

Every call in the Bible contains a commission. There is no vocation without mission. This is also to be found in our passage; Jesus sends Mary on a mission, "Go to my brothers and say to them . . ." (v. 17). Thus she becomes an apostle to the apostles.

Mary's tears had isolated her from everyone else, even from the disciples, who, from the moment she began to weep, she no longer sought to contact. Jesus draws her out of her solitude to send her to his brothers.

If Jesus has pulled Mary up in her fervor ("touch me not!"), it is in order to set her in motion towards others; "Go to my brothers." The arrest of Mary's fervor therefore has a double significance; touch me not because I have to go to the Father; but also, touch me not because you must go to the brothers.

At first sight the passage seems to make a separation apparent between Mary and Jesus; each of them must take a different direction. In fact, this is not so; it is not separation, but communion. In fact, Jesus explicitly chooses words that underscore communion rather than separation. The Father to whom Jesus goes is both his Father and that of the disciples, as he stresses ("my Father and your Father"). Mary and Jesus have the same Father. Those to whom Mary is to go are not unknown or strangers; "go to *my* brothers." Jesus' brothers are also Mary's since they have the same Father. Between Jesus, Mary, and the disciples are true ties of fraternal love, and these ties together constitute a network of fellowship.

This designation of the disciples as brothers also marks a progression in the relationship they have with Jesus. The evening before his death Jesus had already arrived at a new depth of intimacy by telling the disciples that they were no longer servants but friends; "you are my friends" (John 15:14). In what he says to Mary, Jesus is not taking any backward step by calling them "brothers"; on the contrary, he reinforces the relationship by adding that the disciples and he have the same Father. Friends do not have the same Father. Here, the Father is God himself. The disciples are Jesus' friends, but more; they are his brothers.

At no point in John's Gospel had Jesus spoken in this way to the disciples; this is the first time. Never, furthermore, had he said that his Father was also their Father.

There is more. By going to the Father, Jesus is preparing what he had promised his disciples, that is, a mysterious bond of deep fellowship which caused him to tell them, "I go to the Father so that I can be in you and you in me." Mary and Jesus will therefore not be apart. In going to the disciples, Mary will not be separated from Christ but will discover that Christ is in them, mysteriously present in them, and they in him. There is nothing similar to this bond of fellowship except for the bond that unites the Father and the Son ("I am in the Father and the Father is in me"). The flow of love towards the brothers is instinct, inscribed within the flow of love within the Trinity.

The passage concludes with a double use of present tenses; Jesus "ascends" to the Father and Mary "goes" to the disciples. It is the same present time, the same movement of love in the present. When you are with the brothers, I will be there too. When you meet my brothers, I am also there, in their midst, in them and they in me. Only the Risen One can speak like this! He needed to have died and returned to life to be so mysteriously and profoundly present, so profoundly in communion with each one, through the Father, in the Spirit.

The message to convey

Every vocation with a commission contains a message to be transmitted, as is surely the case here. The message Mary is to convey to the disciples is confined to one single sentence, a sentence with the simplest of words, but one that does not cease to provoke our deepest thought today; "I am going to my Father and your Father, my God and your God." All things considered, this is an absolutely extraordinary message.

Why is there such an apparently redundant formula to designate God, "My Father and your Father, my God and your God"? Precisely to attract our attention to the depths of the mystery.

This is not the first time in John's Gospel that Jesus speaks of God as "my Father"; indeed it is very frequent. This manner of speech attracted the wrath of those responsible for religion, who saw in it real blasphemy; by speaking this way, Jesus considers himself to be God, making himself, as a Son, equal with the Father (see John 10:32–33). That really is what it means; in expressing himself in this way, Jesus says he is divine; he is well and truly the Son, the Son of God, even the unique Son of God . . . He should either be stoned as a blasphemer or bowed before and worshipped as the Son.

If the disciples had often heard Jesus say "my Father" with regard to God, they had never, by contrast, in John's Gospel, heard him say "my God"! Biblically, this last manner of speech is just normal in the mouth of each and every member of God's people. By speaking this way, Jesus is affirming his full and total humanity.

Jesus, fully God and fully man; this is the purport of the message Mary is to transmit. This is what the Council of Chalcedon would make explicit against the reductivist theologies which evade one or other of the two natures of Christ; Christ is fully God and fully man.

The Risen One is risen in his full humanity as well as his full divinity.

But Jesus does not stop here; what he adds is another great novelty to the disciples. The words which speak of his divine humanity ("my Father" and "my God") are used again and applied to the disciples; "your Father" and "your God." The perfect balance of terms honors the disciples to the highest degree, beyond every expectation. That the disciples are men, well, fine; but that they might be God . . . !

Rather than gather rocks with which to stone the blasphemer, the church fathers preferred the silent recourse of prayer. Theology has to be worked out in prayer; in prayer the Holy Spirit illuminates the mind, and the contents of the message entrusted to Mary for the disciples are to be received entirely as a gift. In their own nature, disciples are *creatures* of God, but by grace they become the *children* of God, adopted children. This indeed is stated in John's prologue: "to as many as received him he gave the power to become the children of God" (1:12–13).

In order to underline this element of his message, Jesus instructs Mary to impart it to those he is calling for the first time "my brothers." The Only Son of God thus receives his brothers by adoption. To be the brothers of Christ, such is the unfathomable gift on receiving the Risen One, in what is the most humble of wonders. Indeed, the Son becomes man so that purely by grace, men may become children of God, God with them, for them, in them . . . by faith in the Risen One.

The disciples are as human as iron is iron;[5] but immersed by grace in the fire of God, they become fire . . .

I ascend

This first word of the message evokes the ascension, and it is this that John conveys here in the eternal present, unlike Luke who locates it in liturgical, calendar time.

In Luke, the ascension comes forty days after Easter, and Pentecost, fifty days. Here, in John, everything is posited on the same day; it is the actual day of Easter, early in the morning in sight of the empty tomb, when Jesus speaks to Mary of his ascension as an immediate event: "touch me not because I ascend." The evening of the same day, Jesus breathes the Holy Spirit upon the disciples (vv. 19–22). Easter, the Ascension, Pentecost, all belong to the today of Christ, the eternal today of God . . .

In what follows in Luke, the liturgical calendar places this eternal reality into liturgical time. This is the role of liturgy, to take what belongs to eternity and accord it a time of celebration; liturgy is the turning point between time and eternity.

"I ascend to the Father . . ." This affirmation as to the present is truly in the present of eternity. This present time, on the day of resurrection, is the same present we find before Christ's death in his farewell discourse, "I go to my Father" (14:12, 28; 16:28), "I return to the Father" (16:10, 17), and in the high priestly prayer (17:11, 13). These formulations express something already stated at the baptism, where the Son comes up out of the water (Mark 1:10) towards the Father.

---

5. This refers to a figure from the church fathers with a nice twist in the French language. Iron in French is *fer*; fire is *feu*. Thus, *fer* becomes *feu*; iron becomes fire when placed in the fire. (Trans.)

Each of these instances depicts the eternal outflow of the Son's love into the bosom of the Father (John 1.18). The ascension is not the reality of one day, but the outworking of an eternal passionate movement.

"I ascend to the Father." In all the other mentions of the ascension, the verbs are stated in the passive (Mark 16:19; Luke 24:51; Acts 1:9, 11); the Son is "lifted" to the Father. This is the only time in the Gospels where the ascension is spoken of with an active verb, "I ascend." This active verb underlines the free movement of the Son towards the Father; it is of himself, in his own nature, that the Son ascends to the Father.

So, it is in this natural flow of love that the Son is in the Father and the Father in the Son; he both goes towards the Father and he is raised by the Father. It is in the same natural grace that he is in us and we in him, we ourselves both rising towards him and also being raised towards him.

Mary does not answer Jesus; she receives in silence the words of fire before going to pass them on to the disciples; and it thus that the fire has run throughout the earth.

The garden

What are the angels doing in a tomb and Jesus in a cemetery? Should they be in such an unclean place? But are we really dealing with a cemetery? The Evangelist John carefully guards against using the word cemetery and prefers to speak of a "garden." None other of the evangelists speaks in this way. Which garden is in view?

John tells us that the cross is in a garden (19:41), that the tomb is very near, in the same garden, and it is indeed the only tomb in the garden, so that it becomes difficult to think in terms of a cemetery. Moreover, we know that the garden is at The Place of the Skull (19:17), not just any skull but "the" skull, which is to say, not that of just any man, but a man known to everyone. A very ancient patristic tradition, based on a Jewish tradition, considers the man in question quite simply to be the first, Adam; this leads us to think that the garden in question could be the garden of Eden. Was John aware of the ancient Jewish tradition? It is quite possible. From this, John's account takes on a very marked spiritual dimension; Christ dies and returns to life on the very site where the ancestor of all mankind is buried.

The cross is planted in the garden like the tree of life in the center of the garden of Eden. Whoever draws near receives life from the one who hung there. When Christ's side was pierced, water was seen to flow, evoking the river that flowed in the garden of Eden (Gen 2:10).

Was Mary altogether mistaken in taking Jesus for the gardener? Perhaps not! Might he not really be the one who tends the garden?

"Light be!" God said on the dawn of the world's first morning, and light was. Mary enters the garden early in the morning on the first day of the week, in the dawning light. It is the hour when the Father, in silence, ponders afresh the newly created light, while the Holy Spirit hovers over the waters . . . Mary does not seem astonished to encounter angels in the nascent light of the early morning. She turns to see the Living One, then she turns again, as if in an internal dance, to unceasingly contemplate the Well-Beloved.

When he pronounces her name, she begins to speak the sacred language, the language of God in Paradise. Then, in silence, she fills with wonderment . . .

"Why do you weep?" Why indeed? In the presence of the Well-Beloved, the tears become tears of joy.

The prophets had announced this; God himself will wipe away every tear (Isa 25:8). Mary weeps in silence, and in that silence, God himself draws near to wipe away each of her tears . . .

"Touch me not," says the Well-Beloved, halting Mary in her fervency, before leaping forward himself to a new horizon, reviving the fire; "Go and tell my brothers what I have told you . . . of that great love with which we are loved . . ."

Where has your beloved gone, O most beautiful of women?

To which side has your well-beloved turned

That we may seek him with you?

My well-beloved has gone down into his garden, to the beds of spices,

To feed his flock in the gardens and gather his lilies.

(Song 6:1–3)

www.ingramcontent.com/pod-product-compliance
Lightning Source LLC
Chambersburg PA
CBHW032235080426
42735CB00008B/859